Here are the stories of seven unforgettable women from across America. All drastically different, from their personalities and backgrounds to where and how they live.

These are great women. Women who will never be listed in anyone's "who's who", but women who truly should be. They are great, not because of their tremendous accomplishments or glamorous lifestyles but because of their inner strength. Their ability to love. To endure.

Barbara Jenkins will show you America from a viewpoint you won't forget. Come along with her and meet these women...

Ruby — the true western pioneer who journeyed to Texas in a covered wagon. A rare blend of true–grit and gentle femininity.

Jan — the bayou woman with an ear tuned to the subtle sounds of the hearts of others and an incredible story of a personal experience with death.

Lucy Adele — the Idaho princess filled with compassion for others. A woman with nimble fingers that create exquisite needlework art.

Martha — the Tennessee Belle who lives in a one-hundred-and-fifty-year-old plantation house used by the Confederate Army. A widow woman with a sweet southern drawl, a professional flair, and eyes that talk as much as her voice.

Laverne — the country beauty from Illinois filled with stories of an adventurous childhood with five ornery brothers and a heartwarming courtship with a young preacher.

Emma Jean — the shy woman better known as Buckshot who has spent her life hidden in the Rocky Mountains. She has entertained a host of travelers from governors to outlaws.

Betty — the wise Missouri woman who has nurtured a special relationship with her granddaughter, teaching her how to cook on a wood stove and about the important things in life.

(continued on back flap)

I ONCE KNEW A WOMAN

A Patchwork of Seven Unforgettable Americans

Barbara Jenkins

Co-Author of *The Walk West* and *The Road Unseen*

Wolgemuth & Hyatt, Publishers, Inc.
Brentwood, Tennessee

Photographs by Barbara Jenkins

Unless otherwise noted, all Scripture quotations are from the New King James
Version of the Bible, © 1979, 1980, 1982, 1984 by Thomas Nelson, Inc.,
Nashville, Tennessee and are used by permission.

Wolgemuth & Hyatt, Publishers, Inc.
1749 Mallory Lane, Suite 110
Brentwood, Tennessee 37027

Library of Congress Cataloging-in-Publication Data

Jenkins, Barbara.
   I once knew a woman : a patchwork of seven unforgettable Americans
/ Barbara Jenkins. — 1sr ed.
      p. cm.
   ISBN 1-56121-002-1
   1. Women—United States—Biography. 2. Women—Conduct of life.
3. United States—Biography. I. Title.
CT3260.J46 1990
920.72'0973—dc20
[B]   90-46130
                                                CIP

To my precious children
Rebekah, Jedidiah, and Luke

*"Mother, next year when you're
not writing, will you come to more
things at school?"*

*"Mother, once you get done with
your book, will you give me one?"*

*"Mommy, how many more days is
it gonna take you to finish?"*

CONTENTS

ACKNOWLEDGMENTS

THIS BOOK COULD NOT have found its way to the public without help from many people—even the best writers need guidance and encouragement. I am very appreciative of everyone who had any influence, directly or indirectly, in the past year on the development and writing of this book. Although this is a book about women and will be read by both women and men, it would not be in your hands without the following men. I wish to send out big thank-yous to these gentlemen for either their personal encouragement or professional help (of course, there are three women I must mention too):

Ernest Pennell, better known as Ernie and my dependable father, a hardworking retired auto mechanic who fixes my car and the plumbing and thinks it's about time I wrote another book. He told me, "I know what you can do, and how much you wrote in those *Walk Across America* books."

Then there's Bruce. Better known as Dr. Bruce McIver, retired pastor of Wilshire Baptist Church, Dallas, Texas, now an author working on his own book. He said, "This writing is about the hardest work anyone can do. You hang in there." As well as his enterprising wife and my dear friend, Lawanna, who was a sounding board and made helpful suggestions throughout the writing of this book.

Dr. Stanley J. Watson, retired professor from the New Orleans Baptist Theological Seminary, now a busy marriage and family counselor and consultant and a long time friend, mentioned, "This book is a great idea. You're ready to fly . . . "

Frank Pool from San Angelo, Texas, a retired world-hopping industrialist and his lovely wife, Elizabeth, who checked on the progress of this book while flying all over the country. Standing in the middle of the Colorado River trout fishing, Frank said, "You've got the talent. Go forward and don't look back."

Every writer needs someone who is not in the book publishing field to read his or her material and react, honestly, to what has been read. My neighbor, Viki Branchizio, did that for me.

John J. Hollins is a prominent Nashville trial lawyer who wins tough and complicated cases. He encouraged me, "You're a writer, and you'll be happier writing."

Mike Milom, nationally known entertainment and literary attorney from Nashville who guided me through agents and publishers, said, "I think this is an important book because what you're writing about is needed."

Finally, there's Mike Hyatt and Robert Wolgemuth, the editor and publishers of this book. These two men have wanted me to write a book for the past two years. They pursued me as a writer but waited patiently until I discovered them as promising and innovative publishers. One day, I did. And guess what? I believe we're a dynamite team.

To each of you, I thank you for helping me make this book come true.

INTRODUCTION

HERE ARE SEVEN WOMEN to remember from across America, all drastically different, from their personalities and backgrounds to where and how they live. They are like individual pieces in a handmade quilt, each one unique, some quiet and unassuming, some exciting.

There are no helicopter or car-chase scene in their lives. They haven't murdered or sexually abused anyone, nor have any of them lived a double life as an undercover agent or prostitute. They don't take drugs, run with the jet-set, or embezzle money. None of them have been beauty queens, fashion models, or living in palaces. But, clearly, they are survivors who have overcome situations in "real life" that have made them tough and wise.

Those of us in our early forties and younger, namely the baby boomers, have lost sight of such unsung women who have gone before. We have not sat at the feet of older women and learned from them. There's been no time. We're much too busy building our professions, attending club meetings, decorating new homes, running children from one enrichment program to another, buying more and more things, keeping fit at the health club, and trying to be super ladies of the eighties and nineties. We modern women stay well informed watching Oprah

Winfrey, Phil Donahue, Sally Jessy Raphael, and other television talk shows, but we have missed voices like these.

There's an urgent need to hear from these seven women. They help point the way—like lighthouses shining beams through a thick and confusing fog—through the darkness of soap opera affairs, false values, temptations, and non-stop media hype. These women know themselves and what's important. None of these women have been on the cover of *Cosmopolitan*, *People* magazine, or on the front pages of the tabloids. They have nothing to prove, but everything to pass on.

Here are stories where all of us can sit at the feet of experience and look into their long, private lives for a brief moment. The same way a hand-stitched quilt makes you feel warm and takes a long time to create, so it is with these women. Their healthy values are the threads that join them into one. All together, they make a lovely patchwork of womanhood, from a Texas pioneer to a Rocky Mountain woman, to a Southern belle, to a professional health instructor and more.

Get a cup of coffee, sit back in your easy chair, and go with me to meet them. Their front doors are open to us. Some will fascinate you, others will make you feel good, and some will make you wonder how they lived through such hard times. Whatever your reaction to each one, these women will befriend you and challenge you to think for yourself. They are very different from those of us in a younger generation caught up in fast living. They won't be impressed with your money, your fame, your career, or lack of them, but they will show you themselves. They will let you take from them whatever you need to help you along the way.

Chapter One

A Missouri Christmas

THE NIGHT WIND blew hard like a howling madman, whirling sheets of snow mixed with cold sleet, covering the lonely two-lane road, Highway 60 East, making it almost invisible. The solitary car was creeping along at fifteen miles per hour, headlights on dim, the woman driver hoping she would not slide off the road into a ditch, become stranded, maybe freeze to death before anyone found her and her three young children. The windshield wipers flapped back and forth furiously. There were no other cars out this late at night, on Christmas Eve, since most people were already at their destination huddled around a fireplace or exchanging gifts and enjoying the warmth and coziness of home and family.

Suddenly, there was an eerie hush in the sky. That old story of shepherds watching flocks on a cold winter's night many hundreds of years ago, interrupted by a host of angels singing "Peace on Earth, Good Will To Men" was easy to imagine in the quiet snowfall. After all, it was Christmas Eve. Then came another blast of snow-thickened wind, whistling gusts so strong the car weaved back and forth across the road.

"Are we going to make it to MeMe and PaPa's?" The two little boys, Jed and Luke, asked with quivers in their voices from the back seat of the Chevrolet station wagon.

They were scared and worried if they would make it to their grandparents house. The car heater was puffing out air through the vents trying to keep everyone warm, and even the windshield wipers seemed exhausted fighting the storm.

"Mommy, how will Santa Claus find us in Missouri?" little five-year-old Luke asked.

"Can reindeer see in all this snow?"

"Mom? Mom? I wonder how many presents I'll get?" Jed asked. He had just celebrated his seventh birthday and was still excited over the new skateboard he had received for a present.

"I'm hungry," announced Rebekah, the ten-year-old daughter sitting in the front seat. "Mother, do you think I'm pretty? I think another boy at school likes me now," she said in one breath, wide-eyed in the dark. Being a fifth grader, Rebekah thought she was much too grown-up to be worried about reindeer or her little brothers' questions.

"How much farther until we get there?" both boys hollered from the back seat.

Their childish questions were entangled with the deep voice of a radio announcer who was warning travelers across the Midwestern United States about a severe winter storm watch. The temperature would be dropping below an already bitter fifteen degrees.

"The National Weather Service requests all motorists to stay off the highways unless it's an emergency," the announcer said.

"Will you kids be quiet? I can't hear a thing and I need to listen to the weather report!" their mother ordered, turning up the volume dial on the radio. The car groaned across more snow and swerved with the blast of another northwestern wind.

The worried woman tried to hide her fears about the bad weather, keep her three children from knowing how dangerous it was for them to be on the road, steer the car and keep it from slipping sideways into a ditch, and listen to the radio report all at the same time. Her nerves were on edge, tight and strained. The tone in her voice told her children she wasn't in any mood to be patient or tolerant. She had already driven five hours through the grisly night, all the way from Nashville, and her neck was stiff, and her shoulders ached.

"Only forty-five more miles and we'll be there," the woman said with a weary sigh. "We should get there around 10:00 o'clock," she mumbled.

Christmas carols came back on the radio station while the little boys began to fuss over a toy gun in the rear of the station wagon.

"Oh, Holy Night . . . It is the night of the dear Saviour's birth . . ." began playing on the radio. The musical sounds of a church bell tolling and the voice of a sweet soprano singer seemed to calm the tense atmosphere and fill the car with a feeling that they were going to make it to where the grandparents, better known as MeMe and PaPa, would be waiting and watching for them to pull into their driveway. The porch light would be on and inside their house, a new pile of logs would be burning in the wood stove making everything toasty warm and smelling of wood smoke. There would probably be a freshly baked cake sitting on the counter in the kitchen and clean sheets on the beds, hidden under layers of handmade quilts, and certainly, the television would be on, giving up-to-the-minute reports on the weather.

Mile by mile, the car moved slowly through the storm. The clock on the dashboard of the car read 9:50. Almost there. A mean wind was still pounding against the front of the car, but thankfully, the sleet and snow had lessened as the little family inched their way turning south on Highway 67. Strings of colored lights—red, green, blue, orange, and white, some blinking—could be seen off the road, decorating farm houses and becoming guiding lights through the empty and black countryside. The world outside looked as if it was getting ready to pass from a feverish fit into a peaceful sleep.

Ꮹ Ꮹ Ꮹ

There it was. On the ridge of a hill, off to the right was the out-of-the-way gravel road with a tiny cemetery next to it.

As the car turned off the highway onto the rough rocks and frozen earth, the children began jumping up and down.

"This is my most favorite road in the whole wide world," Rebekah sang as beautifully as one of the Christmas carols that had been playing on the radio.

"This old pot-holed road?" her mother shot back with a half grin. "For heaven's sakes, why?"

"Cause it goes to MeMe's house!"

Ꮹ Ꮹ Ꮹ

MeMe's Christmas Day dinner was in the making with sweet potatoes steaming, a fat turkey in the oven, home canned green beans simmering, and other pots of vegetables scattered across the old fashioned wood cook stove. The brand name of the stove was called *Home Comfort* and stood like a massive iron king, taking up one wall in the room. It was white porcelain with four big removable lid burners that could be lifted for more sticks of wood, a large water reservior, an oven for baking, and an ash bin on one side. A wood box filled with split hickory and a black shovel sat at the foot of the stove, almost like servants waiting to be called upon. The stove seemed to command attention and hang onto the glory it had once known from decades past when every home across America used a wood cookstove. This grand old stove had no way of knowing the year was 1989 and not 1929, and that MeMe was really a woman named Betty Jo Pennell.

Betty was now in her early sixties, a medium-sized woman standing around 5' 5", carrying 140 pounds, with silver-grey hair, hazel-green eyes, and delicate facial features. The natural curl to her short hair had stayed all through life and could be seen in her portraits as a young woman when her hair was the color of red chestnuts, long and tumbling with waves. Her refined features, heart-shaped lips and straight white teeth, had made Betty a real beauty back in her early days, and, although she had grown older in years, she still possessed the same charming smile, sparkle, and good looks.

Her country kitchen was busy with food and activity, enough to match the wide variety of home grown herbs behind the cook stove. Thereupon sat an assortment of clear jars lined neatly on open shelves. Each jar was full of either basil, sage, thyme, rosemary, mint, parsley, marigold seed, dried rose petals, lavender, cedar chips, sweet marjoram, red clover, camomile, or even some powdered myrrh. All of the herbs had been planted, harvested, and dried by Betty.

"These are the last of our good sweet potatoes," Betty murmured, lifting the lid to see if they were done.

Rebekah overheard. "I saw a whole bunch of sweet potatoes in a box on the back porch, MeMe," Rebekah said as she danced around the room showing off her new jogging pants and sweater she'd received for Christmas, grabbing a bottled Pepsi, and tinkering with everything in sight. Her youthful energy made it hard for her to stand in one spot for very long. Her long arms and legs made her movements graceful. Rebekah was going to be taller than her grandmother, but she had the same delicate features, curly chestnut-colored hair, and smokey eyes. "That's not what I meant," Betty answered. "Our seed has worn out and these are the last of the crop. We've used this same sweet potato seed for about twenty years and it's just played out—no strength or taste left."

"Hey, here's some of that stuff the wise men gave to baby Jesus," Rebekah said, ignoring her grandmother as she placed the glass jar of myrrh back on the open shelf next to another jar with a bar of old lye soap inside. The jars of herbs were like a still oil painting against the green and gold wallpaper that covered the kitchen walls. All around the room, hanging on the walls were collections of pictures, calendars with notes scribbled on certain days, ceramic and wooden trinkets. One calendar hanging next to the herb shelf had "Preacher, lunch" written across Monday.

Some of the pictures were oils painted by Betty who had a natural flair for art and crafts. There were also wall plaques with different messages. One said, "Listen Paw, when I want your advice, I'll ask U." Another one had a recipe for a "Happy Kitchen" with these ingredients: 4 cups of love, 3 cups forgiveness, 1 cup friendship, 5 spoons of hope, 2 spoons tenderness, 4 quarts of faith, and 1 barrel of laughter.

"Rebekah, come stir this," Betty said as she hustled from one pot to another, giving orders to anyone who passed through the buzzing kitchen and was within helping range. There was much to prepare and all hands were needed.

"What is this?" Rebekah asked, tiptoeing to see inside the stainless steel pan. The wood cookstove was piping hot, and she had to be careful not to lean against it.

"Coconut cream pie filling."

"Is this what you had for Christmas dinner back when you were a little girl like me?" Rebekah asked.

Betty laughed and took a deep breath, trying to collect her thoughts and answer the simple question. How could she explain to her one and only granddaughter the widespread and unbelievable changes since she had been a little girl back during the Great Depression in the early 1930s? A half-century had passed, and life and the world were much different now—so fast, threatening, unstable, materialistic, and people weren't the same. Houses, jobs, schools, towns, churches, nothing was the same, not even Christmas.

"It was hard to have anything for Christmas back when I was your age, much less a fresh coconut cream pie."

"You didn't have anything to eat?" Rebekah asked.

"My mama always came up with something to eat even though we were awful poor. My brothers would kill a rabbit or squirrel, and Mama would make a molasses cake. She'd cook dried apples, sweetened with brown sugar, and put a layer of apples, then a layer of cake, and that was what we'd have for Christmas dinner, and it was good."

The back door slammed, and into the house ran Jed and Luke chasing each other, squealing through the kitchen and bumping into Rebekah.

"Stop it!" she screamed. "These boys are . . ."

"Bang! Bang!" Luke shouted as he pointed his new gun at her. His carrot red hair and shiny blue eyes caught the midday light through the back door. He looked like trouble, standing there with his shoulders squared, legs apart, and pulling the trigger on his plastic rifle, but the deep dimple in his chin and the quick grin on his five-year-old face made him irresistible to grownups, especially women. But, not to his sister, Rebekah.

"Get out of here," she said. "Sometimes I wish I didn't have brothers."

"Huh, I had six of them," Betty laughed. "I was the baby and had all those brothers. We fought like cats and dogs, especially my brother, Glen, who was closest to me in age." Betty's back was turned as she sliced a loaf of homemade wheat bread and heard the porch door slam again. Jed and Luke were about to get a tongue lashing if they didn't quit running through her house. It was bad enough the boys had left empty boxes, torn paper and ribbons, toys, stuffed animals, and clutter everywhere from opening all their gifts. One more chase through her kitchen and those little fellows would be punished.

"Yep, we were always at each other's throats," Glen chuckled as he and his wife slipped through the back door into the room and overheard Betty's remarks. Glen Crain was four years older than his sister, Betty, and lived nearby, just over a few hills and down a curvy road to his small Ozark town in Missouri. He stood over six feet with massive shoulders, and still had a handsome face and head full of gray hair. He and his wife, Sue, had stopped by to see everyone on Christmas Day.

Betty looked back over her glasses with a playful glance at her brother. There were lots of years and memories that passed between them in that moment. Grins and humor were on both their faces. Immediately, Glen and Betty began to banter back and forth like experienced boxers in a ring, punch for punch, but without hitting each other too hard.

"I remember Betty had to sit between MaMa and PaPa at the supper table just to protect her from me," Glen said good humoredly as he pulled out a wooden straight-backed chair and sat down at the antique oak table which was in the middle of the kitchen. He crossed his legs, leaned back on his chair and rubbed his chin. He gently laid his cowboy hat on the table.

Glen had a strong and powerful presence, but he was a warm soul and had a way of drawing kids and adults to his side. Although Rebekah kept stirring the coconut cream pie, she had her ears and eyes glued to this compelling man, her great uncle. Watching Uncle Glen and her MeMe was like watching a sitcom on television or a live play on stage with actors and actresses. They both knew their lines.

Glen started, "Remember one day we walked home from school together, about a mile and half through the woods, and when we sat down to eat supper that night, PaPa asked me what all happened that day?" Glen cleared his throat and paused long enough for everyone to listen, especially his sister. His eyes were aimed in Betty's direction but she ignored him. "I told PaPa what all had happened. Betty and her girlfriend, Ginny, wanted to stop and play, but I was tryin' to get 'em to come on home cause I had to milk the cows, this, that, and the other. Anyway, Betty spoke up and told PaPa, 'Yes . . . and Glen was right behind us . . . just-a-cussin' ever breath!' " Glen said.

"Well! When Betty told PaPa that, PaPa whipped me with a hickory stick for cussin'." He looked over at Betty who was slicing ham. Glen rubbed his chin, "And I don't think I had been cussin' . . . But I can remember those whippin's easier than I can what caused 'em," he grinned.

Betty threw her head back and laughed like a school girl. After all those years since their childhood, she still enjoyed ruffling her brother. Rebekah stood motionless and very quiet, wanting to know more about a hickory stick, but afraid to ask. She just wished her two brothers, Jed and Luke, knew all about one.

The laughter and commotion was like a magnet that brought Aunt Sue, Cousin Bob, PaPa, Aunt Vicky—everyone—crowding into the kitchen where dinner was almost ready, hovering around the table and Uncle Glen. To have a house full of kin-folks waiting for another tale was all Glen needed to prompt more stories and add more spice to the already delicious-smelling room.

He started again, this time telling about two brothers who lived on a farm. Luke's and Jed's eyes got rounder. For the first time, both little boys were not moving. Rebekah looked at her brothers glued to Uncle Glen, but she was still thinking about the hickory stick while she stirred the pie filling.

"These two brothers were always into something, they had knock-down-drag-out fights like any normal family, but their dad was a preacher! Their parents had always been pretty strict with 'em, especially around other people." Glen looked down at Luke who was now sitting in his lap. He couldn't resist those blue eyes and dimple.

"You sure are a pretty boy," Uncle Glen said to Luke.

Glen looked over at Jed and Rebekah with a tender grin to show them his favor too, cleared his throat and continued with the story. "This younger brother was outside, playin' around and seen a rat runnin' around out there by the smokehouse." He stopped. There was a long pause. Glen knew how to keep everyone panting for the next word.

"This other kid, he grabbed a stick, chased that thing and got close enough, and he swung at it . . . And he hit it . . . And he killed it!" Glen said, raising voice to a loud pitch. Everyone was quiet.

"And of course when he did, he just jumped on that thing and stomped it. . . . Just stomped it until its insides came out. . . . And he started to the house with it and came runnin' hollerin' 'MaMa, MaMa . . . Look! I killed that rat, I killed that rat.' "

Jed, Luke, and Rebekah were leaning closer and closer.

"Meantime, another preacher had come and was there in the house. So, this kid came in a-screamin' and a-hollerin', 'MaMa, MaMa, I killed him, I killed him. I stomped that sucker's guts out . . . I killed him!' " Glen was near to shouting as he told this part. He stared at Jed and Luke, and then lowered his voice.

"And the boy looked up and saw the other preacher was standin' there . . . and the boy said to the preacher without blinkin' an eye . . . 'And, he—died—in—the—Lord.' "

The kitchen filled with roars of laughter. Jed and Luke giggled even though they didn't really understand. Rebekah laughed and at the same time was sorting through the meaning, but for sure, she knew it was funny, and it felt good to see all these grown-ups laugh. Some wiped tears of amusement from their eyes.

In her young way, she thought most adults were too serious—always working, making money, worrying about bills, reading the newspaper, rushing from one meeting to another, gone on business trips, going to the doctor, talking about people who were either dying or couldn't find a job, or whispering about someone who had run off with another man's wife. *Why couldn't grown-ups be happy?* To her, it seemed like grownups ought to laugh like this more often.

"I'll tell ya what, Glen. You remember that ol' neighbor preacher we had down in Oxly?" Betty chimed in, not to be outdone by her brother. "He was a huge man, tall and big. Great big anyway you looked at him."

"Oh yeah, Old John," Glen answered. All eyes were on Betty as she bent over the wood stove, pouring hot vegetables from pans into deep bowls. Christmas dinner was only minutes away.

"He had a tremendous voice, really loud, and they said you could hear him from miles away."

"I remember. He always got in a big way of talkin'," Glen added.

"Well, he was holdin' a meeting somewhere, way down in the country. Each family in the church would take the preacher home for a meal. So he went to these people's house who were just as poor as church mice and had a whole gang of kids."

Before Betty could say more, Jed and Luke bounced out of their chairs and ran into the living room to play one of their new games. Their attention span had reached its limit. It was time to be in motion again. Jed started singing "Jingle bells, jingle bells, jingle all the way . . . "

"Like I said, they had a whole tribe of kids," Betty continued as Jed rounded the corner into the next room, and his singing faded. "When the parents and preacher went inside and sat down, all these kids wasn't nowhere to be seen, and there was a bunch of 'em. The grown-ups could hear 'em a-gigglin' and a-gigglin' and directly, one of the kids looked in the window. The kids were outside peekin' in the window at that preacher."

Glen sat with a grin on his face as his memory reeled backwards fifty years. "Well sir, things got real still . . . and quiet," Betty said. "And then they heard one of the boys who was peekin' through the window say to the other one, 'He's a big devil, ain't he?' " Once more, unrestrained wails of laughter, torrential ha ha's from the belly up, filled the kitchen. The outbursts of men and women laughing seemed to wet everyone's appetite. They moved to the dining room to gather around the festive Christmas dinner Betty had prepared with great relish and love.

Rebekah laughed too, feeling very grown-up since she had been the only child who heard this last story. She thought people back in the old, old days seemed more down-to-earth—real, or something. Just like MeMe. Women like MeMe weren't afraid to speak their mind. They didn't worry so much about looking and acting perfect. She wondered all the reasons why MeMe seemed so plain spoken, and why MeMe laughed over unimportant, silly things. Being an urban child, growing up in the homogenized world of the 1980s and 1990s, with designer labels, K-Marts, McDonalds, and country clubs, Rebekah lacked the memory or experience to appreciate the mysteries of her grandmother. Rebekah wondered about the differences, but . . . no matter. Everything felt easy and good.

"And it liked to have tickled Ol' John to death," Betty concluded.

➴ ➴ ➴

The last handful of plates, cups, and saucers from the bountiful meal were stacked away in the cupboard. The houseful of relatives had gone home, and MeMe and PaPa's house was returning to a quiet pace. Jed and Luke had fallen asleep on the living room floor after several rounds of checkers with Cousin Bob. PaPa was snoozing in his easy chair, half-conscious, with one ear awake to hear the 5:30 news on television. MeMe and Rebekah were ready to settle down to their game of "beauty-shop." They played this game every time Rebekah came to visit.

Rebekah would clean, paint, and polish MeMe's finger and toe nails. Then she would take a clean cotton swab and doctor all the little rough places on MeMe's arms and legs. She would rub a layer of skin lotion on MeMe's feet, then do this cycle all over again. The little table beside Rebekah was covered in bottles, nail polish, swabs, scissors, tissue, lotions, and enough supplies to make things look like a real beauty shop. Finally, Rebekah would comb, brush, and style MeMe's hair, sometimes for almost an hour. MeMe loved this part of the game best.

"MeMe?" Rebekah started. "Do you think I'm fat?"

"Good Lord, no!" Betty answered. "You're like a string bean."

"I think I'll try out for cheerleader next year. I made an A on my last spelling test," Rebekah said. She had a way of jumping from one subject to another. "Did you make good grades when you went to school?"

"I went to a one-room country school—Poe School. I only went to the eighth grade cause I despised school. My mama had to make me go every day of my life. I could have gone to high school but I didn't want to," Betty said. "I don't know how I'm as smart as I am." She laughed.

Rebekah giggled and twisted around on her highheels. She wore a pair of old white pumps when she played beauty shop. She loved to prance, dance, click her heels on the hardwood floor and pretend she was a model or famous singer. She separated another lock of Betty's hair, brushing it upwards, and spraying it with a heavy coat of hairspray. Rebekah smiled. Betty's hair was beginning to look like a balloon. "But, I'll tell ya, eighth grade students back then knew more than some college graduates today," Betty snipped. Outside, looking in the window at Rebekah and her grandmother was the fluffy grey-blue cat with four white feet. Betty had named him "Boots."

"Did you have lots of boyfriends?" Rebekah asked.

"There was a neighbor boy, Rommie, who used to walk me home from school, but he was like a brother.

One time we had to cross a creek to get home. There were some stepping stones, and he just hopped across them. I couldn't jump that far, so I asked him to help me. He started to run off and leave me, and I started to cry. He got mad and carried me in his arms across that creek." Betty chuckled. "But, he ordered me, 'Don't you *dare* tell anybody!' "

"We cross a little creek in the car on the way to my school in Nashville," Rebekah said. "But, I'm glad I don't have to walk."

"Oh, it was fun," Betty said. "The road to my school was like a big park. We had to cross by an old home place, and there were plum trees and a big apple orchard where us kids would swipe one or two apples to eat. We had to climb over a rail fence, go through a huckleberry thicket, and sometimes we'd stop and eat rabbit butter in the winter."

"Rabbit butter?"

"That's a moisture that crystalizes and curls around plants. You can find it in low places."

"I could take my lunch to school if I wanted to, but Mother makes me and Jed eat in the cafeteria."

"My mama would pack me a lunch every day. She'd make a dried pie from her biscuit dough, roll it real thin, sprinkle sugar, cocoa and butter on it, bake or fry it, and that would be my dessert for lunch," Betty said. "Ouch!" Rebekah had accidently pulled too hard on Betty's hair. "Take it easy. I'm tenderheaded."

"There's this girl at school. She thinks she's hot stuff, and all the boys like her because she's rich and wears new clothes every day," Rebekah snickered. "She's always bragging about her big house and fancy car. I think it's a Mercedes or Jaguar." Rebekah's modern day concerns were a half-century away from her grandmother's.

"Listen, Rebekah," Betty said, the tone in her voice turned sober, almost angry. "I grew up in an old two-story log house with wide boards on the floors, wood heaters, feather beds, and two dresses to my name. And, my mama sewed them; they weren't ready-made dresses. We were awful poor, and life was hard. We didn't even have electricity or runnin' water. We all drank out of the same dipper instead of crystal glasses. Us kids, we were ashamed of that ol' log house, but we had something most kids don't have today. We had a close family. Everybody looked after each other; people had time for ya. There might not have been much money—no big house. And there was a team of mules—not a car. We didn't have much, but we had a deep love."

Rebekah said nothing. She listened, not fully aware of all her grandmother meant or how that applied to the girl at school who thought she was hot stuff. Yet, Rebekah knew by the fixed look on her grandmother's face and the grit in her voice that her MeMe was saying something important.

"You didn't have carpet?" Rebekah asked.

Betty gently laughed at her granddaughter's reaction. "No-o-o," she said. "But my mama, that's your great grandmother, was real smart and could do anything. Even though she only went to the eighth grade, she was well read, a good cook, an excellent housekeeper, and was an artist. O'course, with eight kids, how did she have time to do anything? But, one year there was no rug on the floor. It was gettin cold and bad weather, so MaMa went to the barn, got some old tote sacks made out of burlap, ripped 'em open, washed 'em, sewed 'em together and made a rug to go on the floor. She got some cloth dye and painted a six inch border of red and green flowers and leaves. That was our carpet. Sure beat puttin' your feet on a cold floor."

"That was my great grandmother?"

"Yep," Betty added, "she was a darling MaMa to me. She never found any fault with any of her children and always told me that when you lose your mother, you lose your best friend."

"Do I really have Indian blood in me?" Rebekah asked.

"Not much, but a little. My great grandmother was a full-blooded Indian. I'm not sure if she was Cherokee or Kickapoo, but yes, she was Indian."

All of a sudden, the telephone rang and interrupted their beauty shop talk. Betty grunted with arthritis as she stood up, reluctantly, from her chair, and shuffled by the kitchen counter lined with crocks of sugar, cornmeal, dried beans, and a clear jar of roasted coffee beans. The telephone was located on the kitchen wall opposite a famous old print of Jesus on His knees, His hands folded together, praying in the Garden of Gethsemane. Directly over the telephone hung another famous print of a poor old man sitting at his table in front of a single loaf of bread, his head bowed, giving thanks. Whenever anyone answered Betty's telephone, they couldn't talk without seeing either Jesus or the old man praying.

Rebekah waited beside the table full of beauty aids while her grandmother talked on the phone. There were many new presents to think about, a new porcelain collector's doll, sweaters, skirts, jeans, two new wrist watches, shoes, a necklace, a microphone, a cassette tape by her favorite rock group—New Kids on the Block—and many other gifts she couldn't remember at the moment. When she returned to Nashville, Rebekah would also be getting a new pair of glasses to wear with all her new clothes. She wondered how she would look in them.

"Since you were so poor, did you get any presents for Christmas when you were a kid?" Rebekah asked. Betty sat back down after a short talk on the telephone with one of her neighbors. She let out a deep sigh. She was tired and ready to stop playing beauty shop, but a few more minutes of having Rebekah rub her legs and feet were irresistible. Since her hair was the size of a football helmet, it was time for Rebekah to work on her legs and feet.

"There were very few presents under our tree, but MaMa always saw to it that we got something. One year my brothers each got a pocket knife and I got a little doll, it was eight-to-ten inches long and looked like a real baby. . . . That was my Christmas."

"You had a tree too?" Rebekah asked.

"We always had a tree," Betty answered. "The boys would go out and cut down a cedar or pine. Here. Let me read this little article that was printed-up in the paper." Betty leaned over and dug through a nearby chest of drawers and pulled out an old clipping. It had turned yellow and was wrinkled. She cleared the frog out of her throat and began to read aloud while Rebekah squirted a fresh blob of lotion on Betty's ankles.

"We didn't have electricity, so didn't know what tree lights were. No way would PaPa have let us put a candle on a tree and light it for fear of setting the house on fire. Mama would supervise the trimming of it. We didn't know what bought decorations were. She would save pretty paper, foil, or whatever she thought would work all year. Once in a while the boys would manage to get a pack of tailor-made cigarettes. They usually smoked Bill Durham or R.J.R., rolling their own. Mama always saved the foil from that, chewing gum, or anything that had foil. She'd draw out a perfect five-point star and put it on top of the tree. She'd make bows and chains from red cellophane and pretty paper. We'd string popcorn and wild red berries. We thought our tree was beautiful." Betty finished reading the article and told Rebekah that she had written that piece for The Prospect-News, in Doniphan, Missouri back in 1984.

"I'm going to be a lawyer or architect when I grow up!" Rebekah announced smartly. She looked feisty. "They make lots of money!" Hearing all those stories about poor people was starting to bother Rebekah. Most people weren't poor anymore. At least, she didn't know any poor people. There weren't any in her private school, church, or neighborhood in Nashville. All her friends talked about designer clothes, vacation spots, and sporty cars. The only poor people she knew were the "homeless" people they showed on television.

"I'm not going to be a writer like my mother, either!" she said.

"Honey, whatever you do when you grow up, I want you to remember this. Now listen to what I'm about to say," Betty looked at her spunky, ten-year-old granddaughter with a loving but piercing stare, her eyes like radar, shooting forth beams of truth. Betty meant business. Her voice had a keen edge of certainty and conviction. She aimed for Rebekah to listen with her heart.

"As you go through life, you're going to learn that money, big houses, fancy clothes, and cars aren't everything. I believe truly . . . truly . . . what is important is to have love and compassion for our fellow man, help others any way we can whether it's financial, just a kind word, listen to them if they have problems, be there, be more understanding or more caring for other people."

Rebekah's eyes became like big globes, round and wide. She felt a twinge. Her pretty freckled face was slightly flushed. She sat silently, rubbing her grandmother's legs.

There was a clear difference between what Rebekah had said and what her grandmother was saying. Here was right and wrong, and MeMe was shining a bright light on what was right. Because Rebekah's heart was still tender, she was able to absorb what she had heard. MeMe's words stung. They were alive.

"I feel at times I didn't learn that early enough in life," Betty said quietly.

ta ta ta

The Chevrolet station wagon was loaded to the hilt. It was time for me and my children to return home to Nashville. There were blankets, pillows, colors and coloring books, bags of candy, apples and drinks, stuffed animals, games, toys, clothes, suitcases, duffle bags, toy guns, puzzles, and more piled and packed throughout the car. There was crawl space left in the rear of the wagon for the boys to play, or stretch out to nap. Rebekah liked to sit in the front seat near me, mostly to listen to the radio, but also to talk about school, her girlfriends, and boys. There was lots to talk and think about as a preteen.

It was a dark, gloomy morning. A light drizzle fell on the station wagon as the last load of Christmas goods were packed. It was a damp cold. Raw. Wet and muddy. PaPa had checked the oil, tires, brakes, antifreeze, and other mechanical parts before my little family hit the winter road home. MeMe and PaPa never said much, but they always worried about me and their grandchildren since I had been divorced three years and was a single parent.

"Barbara got lost ever time she drove those 300 miles to college," my mother, Betty, would laugh. "And, she's still like a goose—wakes up in a new world ever day," she tried hard to make a joke out of my frequent absent-mindedness.

She would say, "The Lord knows Barbara don't have enough sense to raise those kids." Yet, my dear mother gripped her faith in God, like a stubborn Missouri mule, and knew that things would work out. She believed the future held good things and brighter days were ahead.

Jed and Luke threw their arms around MeMe and PaPa, smothering them in kisses. Jed asked for one more cookie.

"You come back and see us now," PaPa smiled at the boys.

Luke climbed in the back and mashed his face and lips against the rear window. "MeMe, MeMe," he shouted. "Can you feel my kisses?"

Rebekah buckled her seatbelt, ignoring everyone. She hated goodbyes, especially when it was goodbye to MeMe and PaPa. Betty leaned through the front door and gave her granddaughter a pat on the leg.

"Thanks for the manicure, hairdo, and making me beautiful. PaPa will wonder who's that strange woman," Betty said, trying to get a giggle out of Rebekah. She pulled Rebekah's little face toward her and kissed her. "We'll be over to see you soon. You be good, and remember I love you."

"Drive carefully!" MeMe and PaPa shouted as the car pulled out of the driveway, turned right, and headed back toward Highway 67. Honks and waves brightened the dreary day and then our station wagon was out of their sight.

ન   ન   ન

The drive back to Nashville usually took six to seven hours and even with the steady drizzle of rain, we should get home by mid-afternoon, before the December dark.

Jed and Luke were occupied with robot games and draw-
ing books in the back of the station wagon. Rebekah was
busy writing in her new diary. This trip would be like all
the others with a rest stop in Kentucky, at the half-way
point, to eat at McDonald's. Traffic would not be heavy
because it was the day after Christmas. Most travelers
would not be returning home yet.

But something was about to happen along Interstate
24, in the middle of nowhere, deep in the countryside of
Kentucky, that would change everything. . . .

"Mother, make Luke stop pinching me!" Jed cried. In
the next moment, Luke wailed like he had been stuck
with a pin. Both boys were fighting, crying, and yelling
when the station wagon started shaking wildly and began
to fishtail back and forth.

"What's wrong?" Rebekah screamed.

"Mommy? Mommy?" The boys yelled.

Unconsciously, I hit the brakes and hung onto the vi-
brating steering wheel with all my strength. Before I had
time to realize there were no other cars on the highway,
the station wagon bolted like a runaway horse, weaving
uncontrollably, back and forth, from the left lane to the
right. The drizzling rain made it hard to know what had
happened. What seemed like hours was only seconds.
Then, the station wagon wobbled and came to a die-hard
stop on the right side of an empty overpass. The right rear
tire had blown.

"Oh, dear Lord," I groaned. I laid my head on the
steering wheel. My hands were shaking as I tried to stay in
control and hide my panic from the children. Rebekah,
Jed, and Luke had no way of knowing how close we had
come to a serious wreck, a head-on collision—if there had
been other cars on the road, probably death—and that

their escape had been a narrow one. They didn't know this, but I did. Now, I was faced with a blown-out tire.

Stooped over in the cold rain, I began to pry the hub cap off the wheel. My hands were stiff and cold and shaking hard. I hoped for the physical strength to turn the lug nuts and lift the tire off the car. But, before that, I first had to figure out how to jack-up the rear of the car. The jack fit under the rear bumper, but it was a mystery to me how to get the thing to work. My thick curly hair was matted and wilted in the rain.

"Mother, what are we going to do?" Rebekah cried. "You don't know how to change a tire, and it's getting dark. There's not even a house around here. Are you going to leave us?" Tears rolled down Rebekah's scared face. Jed and Luke were white with fear. Their little boy eyes were watery as they tried to act brave.

"No, I'm not going to leave you!" I snapped back, agitated. My mind was troubled, since I hated for the children to be afraid, or to see me afraid. I had to figure out something. "Stop that crying right now. Just hush-up and pray!" Meanwhile, I pushed and pried and pulled at the flat tire. Every effort was in vain. It was getting colder and wetter. One or two cars passed by going too fast to stop in the rain. The thought of a pervert or killer stopping to help crossed my mind. I felt stranded and at the mercy of anyone passing by. Here was a single woman and three young children, just like sitting ducks, easy prey for some crazy person to rob, kidnap, even murder. My imagination would have blown apart like the flat tire, had it not been for my intense prayers for help.

"Just ask God to send someone to help us," I hollered to my frightened children inside the car. At least *they* were warm and dry.

Not more than ten minutes passed when a pickup truck with two young men pulled up behind the station wagon and stopped. Their windshield wipers and parking lights stayed on. I kept trying to get the jack hooked on the back bumper, up and under the car, when I noticed I had cut my hand. Down on my knees, chilled and wet, and with a weary sigh, I looked up and saw the two men.

"Need some help, Ma'am?" the driver asked. He wore a cowboy hat, boots, jeans and looked to be in his mid-twenties. The other man looked to be about the same age but wore a farm cap.

"Oh, yes. Please," my mind was racing with an instant evaluation of the men. They looked all right . . . Okay. Their faces were honest. "I don't know how to do this . . . I can't figure out how this works," I said, handing the men the jack.

"Just get back in the car and we'll take care of this," the pickup truck driver said kindly. The men could see how soaking wet and uneasy I was with them. They saw the three children peeking out the window.

In less than fifteen minutes, the two young men had replaced the blown-out tire with the spare. Unfortunately, the spare tire was the modern, "temporary" kind, very small in size and good for only thirty miles. It looked more like an inflated yo-yo than a real tire. Nashville was still 150 miles away.

"You can't make it to Nashville on that thing," the young pickup truck driver said.

"Where's the closest place I can buy a regular tire?" I asked.

"Oh . . . There's nothin' around here," he pondered. "I reckon the closest place is fifteen-to-twenty miles north, a little place called Eddyville."

"How do I get there?"

Both men began pointing, giving directions—turn left here, follow a country road so many miles, turn right, on and on. Of course, they couldn't guarantee if the one filling station would be open. Some businesses were still closed for the holidays. The more they talked, the more confused I became. Three times I asked them to tell me the directions.

"Aw, come on Ma'am, follow us, and we'll take ya there," they said.

Back on the road behind the pickup truck, I and my little family moved slowly down the two lane back road toward the tiny country town in Kentucky. I hoped the one filling station they mentioned was open. What if they didn't have a tire that would fit the station wagon? I had a meager twenty dollars in cash. Then I remembered my credit cards. *If* the gas station was open, *if* they had a mechanic who could work on the car, and *if* they had the right size tire, it would cost seventy-five to one hundred dollars. There were a lot of *ifs*.

But I had reached a point where it didn't matter. My patience, emotions, and nerves were spent and I was still cold and starting to sneeze. There was a big cut on my hand, bleeding, from trying to jack up the car. All three kids were whimpering and complaining, wanting to know when we would get home. It was at times like this I resented being a single parent, carrying total responsibility for three young children.

With a knot in my throat, I turned and looked out the side window, through the dripping rain at the rolling farms and woods so Rebekah, Jed, and Luke couldn't see the tears swelling in my eyes. Just as self pity began to move in and take over, I shook myself down deep on the inside and asked for courage from above. I told myself things would be all right and then let out a weary sigh.

There it was. The gas station. Like an oasis in a wilderness, it was located at the junction of three country roads, and there were two compact cars sitting at the pumps being filled up with gas. Whew! It was open. The two young men in the pickup truck who had led the way, waved and pointed to the station. They kept on driving. I wondered where they were going and wished I could have thanked them for all their time and help.

Inside the garage, I began to explain my troubles to the gas station attendant and mechanic. Both men were around fifty years old, one short and the other tall and burly. The shorter man appeared to be in charge, wiping off black grease that coated his thick hands. He was using a shop towel. He wore a grey coverall work suit and light weight jacket. He had smart blue eyes, dark skin with deep creases, and kept a cigarette hanging out of the corner of his mouth. Trails of smoke went upward, making him keep his left eye half shut. For a second, he looked like an outlaw. Both of these men had tough, surly ways and acted like they chewed nails for fun.

"We got one tire left that'll fit yer car," the short man said. He was gruff. *This is going to cost a mint,* I thought. He told the tall man to get the tire off the rack and begin work.

It was getting later and later, almost 4:00, colder, and the kids were hungry. One hour had already passed, then another as the rough men worked. They struggled by hand to get the blown-tire off the rim, huffing and puffing and swearing under their breath. For some reason, they didn't have the right piece of equipment to automatically remove the tire off the rim so they had to do it manually. Meanwhile, I tried to entertain Jed and Luke who had found a mud puddle and couldn't resist walking back and forth through it. Rebekah buzzed around inside the gas station office looking at the bawdy calendar that hung over the cash register. There was a picture of an almost-nude woman on the cover.

"Mother, did you see that calendar?" Rebekah whispered.

"Yes, honey."

"Boy, I'm never gonna wear anything that skimpy," she said.

"I hope not. Some things are supposed to be private," I murmured in a hurry. This was not exactly the time or place to talk about virtue. My thoughts were geared toward getting the tire fixed, driving home safely to Nashville, and how much all this would cost. I had visions of the bill adding up by the second. Fixing this tire was taking forever. This kind of labor wasn't cheap either. What if they didn't take a credit card? There was no doubt the bill would be a minimum of one hundred dollars.

At long last, the short man walked back into the office, his jaw locked around a new cigarette. He was wiping his grease covered hands again. There was steel in his eyes.

"Got 'er fixed," he said. His voice was muscular.

I took a deep breath and asked bravely, "How much do I owe you?" Jed and Luke were already back in the car. Rebekah stood beside me waiting to hear his answer.

"Well . . . Let's see here . . ." His words hung in the air. He was probably having trouble adding up all the figures in his head.

"That'll be three dollars for the used tire and four dollars labor."

"Wha-a-a-t?" I shrieked.

"Seven dollars in all . . ." he added.

"That can't be right. I owe you more than that!"

"It's Christmas!" he said frankly.

"But, but you worked over two hours, and . . ."

"It's Christmas." he said again. His voice was flat, without emotion.

"I don't feel right, please let me pay you more," I urged.

"It's Christmas!" He said with finality.

&ea; &ea; &ea;

Back in the station wagon right at dark, smiling and feeling like another storm had passed, my little family resumed our journey home to Nashville. We were driving down a narrow zigzagging road toward Interstate 24, this time following the burly tall man from the gas station in his pickup truck. Again I had to ask three times for directions back to the highway. When I did this, the mechanic shook his oil-streaked head and said to follow him.

"I'll take ya to the interstate," he said.

Rebekah and the boys cheered and waved goodbye to the tough mechanic as he pointed out his window and through the cold drizzle to the ramp leading onto the interstate. He drove away in the other direction. A sparkle returned to Rebekah's eyes and a big grin crossed her lips. She flipped the radio dial on, playing pop tunes. Jed and Luke were already scuffling in the rear of the station wagon and everything was back to normal. All was well.

Then Rebekah remembered something. She could hear MeMe's clear voice, those arrow-like words all over again, back when Rebekah was rubbing MeMe's legs with lotion . . . *I believe truly . . . truly . . . what is important in life is to have love and compassion for our fellow man, help others any way we can . . .* The words echoed in Rebekah's heart.

Just as another top ten song bounced on the radio, Rebekah decided she would tell MeMe all about this next time they played beauty shop.

BETTY'S COUNTRY CORNBREAD

Ya have to have an iron skillet; there's no other way of makin' cornbread without an iron skillet. Put that skillet on, and you let it get hot. I use oil because I have to watch fat intake. I put two tablespoons oil or one pat of oleo in that skillet and get it good and hot.

Mix two cups of self-rising cornmeal. Use a good grade of white cornmeal, a half teaspoon baking soda, buttermilk and one egg. I make the batter thin. You pour it in that hot-piping-sizzling-hot skillet.

You put it in a 400 degree oven, and you bake it fast! When it comes out, it's brown, crusty, and good.

ta ta ta

Chapter Two

Buckshot in the Rockies

Excuse me, please . . . Excuse me, please," the CBS camera man said, trying to be polite.

The camera man repeated his request over and over as he pushed his way through the crowd and motioned for one spectator to move out of the way so he could film the group of scientists huddled on the ground. Swarms of people were standing around. A crowd of over one thousand spectators were straining their necks to see what was happening. There was a bright yellow plastic banner that separated the eager watchers from the investigators. It read, "CRIME SCENE—DO NOT CROSS."

"Did he really *eat* five men?" one woman gasped.

"I heard he shot one man and ate four," another woman whispered.

"Look! They found a skull." There was a steady hum from the people talking in hushed tones while anxious reporters fired questions at the team of archaeologists and forensic pathologists who worked quietly. They brushed away dirt and carefully handled an assortment of body parts from a shallow grave only thirty-two inches deep. The bright sun was high in the Colorado sky and made people squint their eyes and camera men close their camera lenses to keep out the glaring light. This warm July day made the snow-capped mountains resemble ice cream cones with millions of glistening crystals. Like a castle wall, up and around the crowd of people were five dramatic, silent mountains, all reaching over 14,000 feet. They towered over the tiny village of Lake City located in the heart of the San Juan Mountains in southwestern Colorado. Uncompahgre Peak stood as the giant at 14,309 feet. Weatherhorn, Red Cloud, Handies, and Sunshine peaks were nearby watching too. All of these gigantic mountains had kept the secrets to this legendary case for 115 years.

Would the team of scientists find the truth? What really happened during that treacherous, snow-blown winter in 1874? Flamboyant tales had been told for over a century about the six men looking for gold who took off in midwinter guided by Alferd Packer with a week's supply of food, headed over the San Juan Mountains to the Los Pinos Indian Agency when deep snow forced them to travel along the top of the mountain. Then a glacial snowstorm hit. It was February. Cold. Forever freezing. Probably fifty below zero. They traveled about ten days in a blinding blizzard and lived on rosebuds and pine gum. Some of the men were praying, some crying, and one man was said to have gone crazy, but they were all starving to death. When that summer of 1874 arrived, five corpses were discovered a short distance from the Continental Divide below Lake San Cristobal. The prospector who accidently came upon the decaying bodies said: "It was a ghastly sight to see five men who had been butchered in cold blood. . . . The flesh had been cut off from four of the bodies about the breasts, thighs, and calves of the legs. The fifth body, an old man with frosted hair, was only robbed of a little flesh from his thighs. . . . "

Nine years passed before Alferd Packer was captured in the Wyoming Territory, and colorful court trials, stories, and legends about this mild-mannered, soft-spoken man filled the newspapers from coast to coast and played on the imaginations of the readers. But people who knew Alferd Packer said it was incomprehensible that such a kindly man who loved children and laughed easily could have killed and eaten five human beings. His guilt or innocence became an ongoing saga.

The sensational trial in Lake City ended when the judge read his decision, and Alferd Packer became the only man convicted of cannibalism in the history of the United States: "You, Alferd Packer, sowed the wind, you must now reap the whirlwind . . . the memory of you and your crimes will fade . . . With God it is different. He will not forget, but will forgive. He pardoned the dying thief on the cross. He is the same God today as then, . . . a God who tempers the wind to the shorn lamb, and promises rest to all the weary and heartbroken children of man, and it is to this God I commend you. . . . "

Although the evidence was circumstantial, Alferd Packer was sentenced to hang, but he claimed his innocence to the end. Even though the judge said the memory of Alferd Packer would fade, standing here under the blue Colorado skies more than one hundred years later, people were still remembering and wondering. The nagging question remained: Did Alferd Packer kill and eat his companions?

Most modern day Americans had never heard of Lake City, Colorado until now. Reporters from Baltimore, Washington, D.C., New York City, Los Angeles, and Chicago were scribbling notes and sticking microphones in front of the team members who were exhuming the bodies for scientific study. Television crews from ABC, CBS, and NBC were there. *National Geographic*, *People* magazine, and *U.S. News* collected information. Radio stations re-corded. Telephones, fax machines, satellite equipment, and cameras appeared like bees searching for pollen.

But none of the reporters noticed the shy mountain woman standing at the edge of the crowd who had long ago been nicknamed *Buckshot*. Her real name was Emma Jean. She wore a faint grin across her lightly colored red lips as she stood, watching with knowing eyes and folded arms. Her hair was short with auburn highlights, and she wore denim jeans and a lightweight denim jacket and boots. She looked to be in her fifties instead of seventy years old. In her western gear, she was slim and petite and mysteriously beautiful against the blotchy brown hills and green pines.

Emma Jean's deep blue eyes were as clear as the overhead sky as she silently watched with caution and interest. This splash of publicity would soon be over. The journalists would fly away, and things would return to normal for her and her husband, Perk Vickers, and the hundred or so other residents who worked hard to live here. Emma Jean knew better than the scientists or the reporters how these beautiful and rugged San Juan Mountains were breathtaking to look at, but fickle when it came to letting people survive. She knew because she had lived across the road from this grave site most of her life and had been in these mountains longer than any other woman alive. Emma Jean Vickers was the last pioneer woman in this frontier mining town.

ё ё ё

"I cremated the bacon," Emma Jean chuckled under her breath. Her early morning voice was low and husky. She pulled a platter of black bacon out of the microwave and shook her sleepy head. She shuffled across the kitchen floor of her sixty-year-old hand-hewn log cabin in fuzzy house slippers and coughed. She sipped a mug of steaming coffee. Her blue eyes weren't wide awake yet because she was not a morning person and usually did not eat breakfast unless her husband, Perk, was fixing one of his famous sourdough pancake breakfasts for guests. Emma Jean poured me a cup of fresh brewed coffee and asked if I wanted some of her rose petal jelly. It was clear pink and actually made from roses.

I was sitting at the round oak kitchen table with blue checkered placemats in front of me. Napkin rings held real cloth napkins, not paper ones. They were blue too. Emma Jean's favorite color was blue which was understandable because of her blue eyes and auburn hair and fair skin tone. Her breakfast table looked formal and feminine next to the wood paneled walls where a brown elk hide covered most of the wall behind me. The hide must have been seven feet long and five feet wide. There were signs of mountain life and the wild west everywhere I looked. Enlarged glossy photographs of hidden lakes and wild flowers hung next to the elk hide. Giant liquor bottles from old-timey saloons were collected across the top of the cabinets, and thick coyote hides made me want to have a fur coat.

"Hey!" Perk spoke into the telephone. He joked, "this is Vicker's Breakfast Grill and it's gonna be officially closed in about fifteen minutes." Perk Vickers was a feisty, blue-eyed native Colorado man who looked sixty years old instead of seventy-five. He was excitable and laughed a lot, and swore a lot, but he loved people as much as he did these mountains where he was born and had lived his entire life. "Are ya comin over?" Perk asked. He was talking to his daughter Peggy. She and her nine-year-old son, Garrett, also lived on the spread-out Vickers Ranch, down a gravel road, and across two trout ponds and a swift river that ran through the middle of the ranch. Her place was nestled in a grove of pines. Whenever Perk fixed a batch of his pancakes, all the family and anyone who wanted to join in was invited.

Emma Jean gazed out the wide bay window that surrounded the breakfast table to see who was coming. She had blooming red geraniums and lush green house plants sitting on the window ledge soaking up the morning sunshine. The greenery created a perfect boundary for the natural view through the bay window. The view out this window, as well as every other window in her log cabin, was pure titanic mountains and endless blue skies. "That Paul . . ." Emma Jean mumbled to herself and grinned with pride. "He's the best lookin' and sweetest kid." She was talking about her tall, blonde-haired, college-age grandson who strolled in the back door of the log cabin with two ranch dogs, "Partner" and "Nellie." The dogs wagged their tails and barked at Perk while he stood over the electric stove flipping thin pancakes up in the air. His sourdough pancakes were as light as a feather and about the size of a saucer. Perk expected everyone who ate breakfast to eat at least fifteen pancakes each. For anyone who couldn't handle that many pancakes, the tongue-dripping and smiling dogs were glad to help out.

Following close behind the dogs were Paul's dad and mom, Larry and Paulette Vickers. They also lived on the big alpine ranch, just across a dusty driveway and up on another hill. They lived within walking distance. Emma Jean's log cabin was getting fuller of people and dogs by the minute, but she seemed to bask in the flood of activity. Having family and friends around pleased her. She admired them all as she darted her quiet mountain eyes from one to another. She was checking to see who had eaten and who had not. She cleared her throat several times, waiting for the right moment to break in the clatter of conversation. Emma Jean was not obtrusive, even with her own children.

"How about some breakfast?" Emma Jean asked quietly during a two-second pause from the barking dogs and outbursts of laughter over Perk's jokes. She was speaking to her only son, forty-three-year-old Larry, who had taken charge of most of the Vickers Ranch operation and tourist business since Emma Jean and Perk planned to travel and lighten their work loads. Although she and Perk didn't look, act, or feel their age, they were glad to have Larry and Paulette share the business.

Larry was busy thumbing through the pages of the telephone book and said he had already eaten. He needed to make a business call. Emma Jean turned and handed the platter of burned bacon to handsome Paul to eat with his stack of pancakes. Paul was hungry and his over 6' tall, youthful body could handle all the pancakes and eggs. Paul ate fast.

Each of the Vickers had jobs to do after breakfast. Paul and his dad were headed to Montrose, hauling a fifth wheel trailer to Paul's sister, Faith, who worked as a full time sheepherder with her husband. They needed this trailer to live in during lambing season. That meant two hundred to three hundred lambs might be born each day, and sheepherders had to be on hand day and night. While Paul and his dad were hauling the trailer, Paulette was going to paint a horse corral fence down by the barn. Everyone worked around here.

"Anyone want any more pancakes?" Perk hollered across the crowded room. "Come on, Barb, you can eat three or four more," he laughed at me from the stove. He had fresh yellow eggs frying in an iron skillet, popping in hot bacon grease. Emma Jean drank more coffee, and her warm eyes were coming awake. Perk wanted to know if I could eat another egg. My stomach was bloated with the ten saucer-sized cakes I had already eaten. One more bite of anything and I would explode. I already worried if I would be able to bend over to shift gears in the jeep.

"Here ya are, Buckshot," Perk bounced over to Emma Jean and handed her a plate full of lightly brown cakes. She lowered her eyes, cleared her throat, and thanked him. Her voice trailed off in a hoarse whisper. Even with Perk, her husband of forty-five years, she was unpretentious. It was moments like this when Emma Jean reminded me of the deer that roamed the timbered highlands around her cabin. Deer were shy, sensitive creatures, slight and tender, but still sturdy and able to survive in this rugged country. Deer had a reserved strength about them. Emma Jean was like that, a curious mixture of being strong but very soft and tender. Perk had nicknamed her *Buckshot* years ago and whenever he talked about her, his chest swelled out and his eyes danced. "If Emma Jean did the most wonderful thing on this earth, she'd be so modest she wouldn't stand up and be recognized," he teased, patting her on the shoulder as he walked back to the stove to flip another set of pancakes.

"Oh my gosh," Emma Jean muttered in a low, hoarse voice. Without makeup or lipstick, her face turned red.

"I'll tell ya. I'm not a damn bit modest," Perk announced. "I've been kicked in the rear end so many times in my life that if I get recognition for something I've done, then I think I'm deservin'."

Just then, the telephone rang and Emma Jean answered. After all the strong coffee, sour dough cakes, and compliments from Perk, she sounded more energetic. At last she was awake, and a slow smile crossed her face. It was Betsy, a lady friend from town who ran an art-to-wear, specialty clothing store. With only a hundred or so Lake City residents, there were no customers, and business was at a standstill this time of the year, so Betsy and other town women played cards. Emma Jean loved to play bridge. Men played poker, and the ladies played bridge. A hot game was set for later in the day, somewhere downtown, and I was invited.

Downtown Lake City was not Chicago or Denver or Dallas. This mountain town sprang up during a gold rush boom between 1876 and 1881 and still had the look and feel of a gamblin', whiskey-drinkin', pistol-packin' town. During the gold digging years, Lake City was full of hundreds of rough miners and cowboys who found their way through the mineral rich mountains and wandered into this town, nestled under the peaks, sitting at over 8,000 feet and hidden from the rest of the world.

But after the turn of the century and Prohibition, the miners' money was gone, and the town dwindled to what it was today—a couple of hardpacked dusty streets with a wooden walkway in front of the Lake City Drug Store, the First National Bank, a small medical center, and Timberline Craftsman gift store. There were some tourist cabins, a post office, four small churches, one open cafe, and several century-old Victorian houses with curly lattice work on the porches. The Silver Street Saloon and Boo's Saloon were meeting places for the local people. Boo's Saloon had just opened and was across the road from the city park where children played while their parents talked to storekeepers, or to the nurse, or had a beer.

Emma Jean's log cabin was only two and a half miles from town and Betsy's clothing store. The way to get to town was down a narrow, curving road, Highway 149, that snaked through deep canyons and sharp cliffs that dropped hundreds of feet to an icy river. There were no guard rails on the side of the road into town, and driving a jeep was fun unless the brakes were bad or you got too close to the edge of the road. It was a long, long way down.

"Okay, hon. We'll see ya soon," Emma Jean cooed. She hung up the telephone and nodded at me.

"Well, I don't know . . . " I hesitated. Back in my college days, I had played some bridge but had forgotten everything. I felt inadequate and reluctant, and sort of stupid. It had been too many years, and I couldn't remember much about the game, and I certainly wouldn't be a good card partner.

Emma Jean's blue eyes gave me a double-take. "Anytime we can get four people who can hold thirteen cards, then we got a game." She never cracked a smile. "Sometimes, it doesn't matter if you can talk." Laughing, I threw my head back and told her if a warm body was all they needed, I could manage that. This gentle frontier woman nicknamed *Buckshot* tickled me. More than once her quiet spicy side would jump out and surprise me. That must have been one of the reasons Perk fell in love with her so many years ago and brought her back to these mountains.

ả ả ả

After breakfast, Emma Jean appeared through the living room doorway of her cabin dressed like a trailblazer in blue jeans, black and white fur boots, and a denim jacket that would have stopped fashion designers in New York or Los Angeles. It had drawings all over it and was a pictoral history of Emma Jean's life in these mountains. There were wildflowers, the state flag, a hummingbird, a horse, her log cabin, and even Emma Jean's wedding date in 1945 with a clear drop stone to symbolize her engagement ring. A long leather tassel hung on the right shoulder and looked perfect with her tassel-beaded earrings made from real porcupine quills. The earrings hung to her shoulders. Emma Jean reminded me of a "white sister" to the Ute Indian squaws who lived in these same San Juans long before her. This outfit was right for Emma Jean, right for these mountains, and no woman could have looked more like the western frontier than she did at that moment standing against the enormous old logs in her living room. I couldn't help but stare at her. She was something to behold.

"Oh, Emma Jean, you look terrific!" I cheered. I wondered how she stayed so trim and petite. There were young women in their twenties who didn't look as stunning as she did at seventy. "What do you do? Jane Fonda aerobics?" I teased her.

"Ummmm . . . well," she thought a second, "I iron every morning."

The colors from Emma Jean's blue jeans and jacket and the old spruce logs blended together and were moody and rich in the shafts of morning sunlight that came through the window. Tiny dust particles hung in the streams of light. The logs were golden with age and had hints of red, brown, and orange. With pride, Emma Jean had told me these logs had been split and chopped by Perk back in 1929 when he built their cabin and in the same year, he shot the massive bull elk on the wall over the fireplace. It was the largest elk head I had ever seen in all of my travels across the West. It had a twelve point rack of antlers, and a beard cape that hung a couple of feet down below its neck.

In slow motion, Emma Jean told me about the fireplace underneath the big elk. It was made out of flat moss-covered rocks gathered from around here and built by a man named Floyd who had been in the penitentary and was given to explosive tantrums and a dangerous temper. The long wooden mantel over the fireplace was another story that she'd tell me later. The mantel was loaded with Colorado relics. There was a small stuffed animal (either a weasel or martin), on one end of the mantel and a bowl of precious ore rocks and metals from the mines sitting on the other end.

"When we married, all we had was this one room," Emma Jean explained, "And we didn't have very good roofs, and one day it came a big rain." She pointed to the open beamed ceiling with the massive logs stretched across the entire length of the room. "Oh, ya never saw anything like it. The roof was leaking and ol' Norman, this visitor from Oklahoma came over to see me." Emma Jean paused as she remembered just how it happened. "I owned three pots and pans . . . and had them sittin' around catching the pourin rain, . . . and . . . ummm . . . ol' Norman said don't worry about it; I can fix that leak in a minute." Emma Jean looked out the front window at the clear sunny day, and a ray of light caught the twinkle in her blue eyes. She was remembering, but she kept her facial expression the same. Her voice stayed slow and steady. "Ol' Norman pulled out this .44, aimed it down at the floor, and shot right in front of me . . . a hole about the size of a toothpick and said, 'Don't worry, the rain will go right through there.' " Emma Jean chuckled. She stood quiet for some time then raised her eyebrows. "Of course, it just drained and drained."

Looking out the living room window was like looking at nearly fifty years of this woman's life. I could see most of the Vickers mountain ranch spread out over a green oblong valley with snow peaks all around. It was postcard perfect. At the far south end of the valley was the Alferd

Packer Massacre Site where all the publicity and media crews had been the day before. Horses grazed in fertile pastures, and beaver had built tree-trunk dams upstream in ponds off to the side of the clean river that divided the Vicker's property in half. Long-haired cattle got fat on upper pastures.

"Yes, it was rough," Emma Jean said without regret. "Rather primitive. It was a new life . . ." Her voice filtered away softly. Remembering all the years in this scenic valley was not as pretty as it looked. There had been many years of snow-bound blizzards and harsh winters at forty below zero, long stretches of isolation, hard to get in or out of Lake City, and no way to make money. When she came here there was no electricity, no televisions or telephones, no paved roads, no indoor plumbing, no running water, no modern conveniences, no doctors or nurses—nothing except austere beauty. The pure air and unspoiled country were rewards enough, but in order to enjoy their over-whelming wonder, there had to be food on the table. And that meant physical work and living without comforts.

"We had no refrigeration, per se, just old wood iceboxes. So we cut ice off the ponds in winter time to keep food through the summer," she said. "In the winter, we could keep our meat outside, and it would freeze solid, of course."

There was a general store in Lake City that carried everything from miner's lamps to wool socks. Whenever local men killed extra elk or deer, they took the fresh meat to the store to be sold along with the beef or pork on hand.

"When I'd go to the store, Henry Hoffman would say, 'Let's see, there are four-or-five in your family? You can have five pork chops cause I have to save some for the others,' " Emma Jean remembered. However, when it

came to filling her cabin cupboards for the long and bit-
ter-cold winters, Emma Jean had to journey the fifty-seven
miles one way out of the 14,000 foot mountains and down
to Gunnison, Colorado which was the closest town. Gunnison had about five to six thousand people but to get
there was a major undertaking.

"It was a gravel road and wasn't too bad in the winter
if you got behind the caterpillar that opened the road,"
she explained. As an afterthought, she remembered,
"There was an old miner on his way home to Lake City.
He slipped off in the ditch, and the snowplow found him
dead the next morning."

She told me it was even tougher to make the trip to
Gunnison in the spring because the frozen gravel road
would begin to thaw out in the warm sunshine. Although
she and Perk had a car back then, there were no four-
wheel-drive vehicles, and traveling was not easy. It took a
long time and a lot of effort.

"You left early, before the sun came out and while the
road was still frozen. You came back to Lake City when
the road froze after the sun went down or you'd be buried
in mud," Emma Jean said. "It was a two-and-a-half hour
trip each way, and if you got stuck, hopefully you could
help yourself or someone would come along."

While the two of us stood in her log living room, I felt
like this was a scene from a storybook. There were many
unseen tales to be told, and her faraway glances told me I
had only scratched the surface. How had she endured all
these years, hidden away up here? I wished to know more
as I watched her daydream. I felt like a miner digging in
these hills for gold. Would I find the answers? Contrary to
the rugged Rockies where she had lived most of her life,
Buckshot had a genteel streak and elegance about her. I
could see it in her proper diction when she spoke, her flair

with clothes, and her good manners. She was a charming mystery.

Although I had known Emma Jean since October, 1977 when, during the long walk across America, I had hiked over Slumgullion Pass and stopped here on her ranch to live for the winter, she was still an enigma. We used to sit and drink coffee together on dark winter afternoons and watch the grey skies turn into snow while the men fed cattle, but she had never really told me much about her roots, her childhood, or where she came from.

All I knew about Buckshot was this: She was from Texas, and first met Perk when she was seventeen years old on a summer trip to the mountains and married him about eight years later. Drinking coffee together back in 1977, Emma Jean didn't talk about herself but instead, wanted to hear me jabber about my adventures walking across America. Young and full of energy, I obliged and talked her ear off. Since then, I had mellowed and done some maturing and felt like I needed to understand more about this mountain woman I once knew. For my sake, I needed to know her deeper and better. Perk was right. Emma Jean was modest, and I felt honored when she told me more about herself.

"Yeah . . . I came along kind of late. I don't think my parents were . . . shall we say, expecting me?" she said, amused.

Buckshot was born on a three-hundred acre farm west of Fort Worth in a little place called Thorp Springs, Texas, and she was the last of eight children. They farmed oats and cotton, and raised chickens, milk cows, and some cattle. They had one horse. Her mother was a school teacher and her father a farmer. Several of her relatives were college professors, and one aunt, called Aunt Bessie Hale, was the poet laureate of the Southwest.

Emma Jean was given piano lessons and encouraged to study and get an education. She walked to Cactus Hill School that had a big wood stove and outdoor toilet. "I would walk cross country about a mile and a half to school and had to go through a pasture. There was a bad bull in there who would take out after me, so I hid when I saw him coming," she recalled.

Growing up, Emma Jean also helped her mother hoe a big garden, can fruit and vegetables all summer, and she rode the horse. Her family went to the Church of Christ in Thorp Springs. Going to church was her primary social life. "It was always a big, big thing to get to go anywhere and visit people of my age. Parents didn't run their children around all over the country just to visit, so . . . ahh . . ." Emma Jean was pulling at her memory from sixty years back.

"I had a lot of fun at home with my brothers and sisters, and we played card games. As a child, cards were entertainment because we didn't run down to the zoo or go see someone."

Bingo! Now at long last, I understood why Emma Jean had such a love for cards and for playing bridge, but I wondered if her childhood preacher or church doctrine approved of cards. In those days, many churches objected to going to the movies, smoking cigarettes, drinking liquor, and playing cards because they believed such things were from the devil.

"Oh, heavens no!" Emma Jean said. "We played every kind of card game that ever has been." Then, under her breath she added, "But my sister got some piano music called 'Red Hot Mama.'" Emma Jean half grinned at me, "My daddy burned that music."

She was reserved about her faith and reluctant to talk about religion, yet tolerant of people who held beliefs different than hers. She had grown up in the Church of Christ, but after graduating from high school and working in Fort Worth, she joined the First Christian Church. Then, when she married at age twenty-five and came to these majestic but isolated mountains, only one church stayed open during the snowbound winter. So, Emma Jean became a Presbyterian. She had learned how changing circumstances and location had a lot to do with where a person attended church.

"I like parts of them all," Emma Jean pondered. "I think religion is necessary in your life. There are many differences." In her thoughtful manner, she peered toward the snow-peaked mountains where she had looked for almost half a century, drawing some kind of lasting strength and wisdom from them. Then she looked down. Her thoughts were her own. I waited. The cabin was perfectly still except for the fingers of sunlight through the window, warming potted green plants on the floor near the fireplace. In a moment or two, she raised her eyes to mine and looked at me with sky-blue purity.

"I think probably one of our worst faults is judging other people, don't you?" she asked.

ਣ ਣ ਣ

The motor on the yellow Toyota jeep was running. The jeep was parked on the edge of a hill in front of the log cabin, waiting for Emma Jean and me to hop in and take off to town. Perk had started the jeep for us and gave me last minute warnings about how to shift the gears, to drive carefully, and to watch out for deer. He treated me like a daughter and had a way of taking care of everybody. He chuckled over the old horse shoes lying on the floor of the jeep and asked me if I needed any. He threw them in the rear.

Like the Lone Ranger and full of confidence, I jumped under the jeep's steering wheel ready to drive off on a dusty trail. However, when I pushed down on the clutch and the gas pedal, the jeep jerked, sputtered, and fought me. The gears grinded when I pushed at the stick shift in the floor. My stomach, full of sourdough pancakes, took a flip-flop, and I cringed. *Uh oh*, I had to do better or Perk wouldn't trust me in these mountains with his jeep . . . or his Buckshot. He shook his head and hollered.

"By God, Barb, you can do better than that," he said. "I'll guarantee ya can." He stood there like a cheerleader.

Emma Jean calmly told me to take my time, and there was no hurry. She leaned out the window and told Perk we'd meet him at the cafe in town for a bite of lunch, and that she was stopping by Wayne's place to have her hair combed. Wayne ran a small shop in Lake City.

"What are you going to the beauty shop for?" Perk asked. "You don't need no fixin' up!" There was a warm-hearted look on his face.

In a rugged way, this was a compliment as free and natural as the outdoors. Perk was like that—unpolished and full of instant humor and good will toward people, often sprinkled with saucy talk. Emma Jean gave Perk a husky laugh and we were off, down the steep driveway that overlooked the valley and ranch. I pushed the brakes to the floor and looked both ways. The jeep screeched to a halt as I worked the clutch, brakes, and stick shift.

"Are you easily scared?" I mumbled, pushing and pulling at the gears to keep from sliding off the hillside.

"Naw," she said.

"Have you ever been afraid?"

A blank look came across her face. "Ummm, I'll have to think about that," Emma Jean answered. "I'm sure I have. . . . "

Across the road, past the ponds, and over the rapid river, dotting the hillside under a row of mountains were twenty little log cabins. They were used for vacationers from June through September each year, and this was the Vickers Ranch sixty-first year in the tourist business.

Perk had told me at breakfast, "Here ya got a very short time to make a livin' and when the tourists leave in the fall, she's over with, and hell–we're eatin three meals a day, drivin' cars, and expenses go on, and taxes goes up." It was under those log cabin roofs Emma Jean had spent most of her mountain life—cleaning, changing bed linens, scrubbing, and working to help make money, and hang onto the ranch. How many tubs of towels and sheets had she washed and hung out to dry in the blowing valley winds over the years? Survival here was not climbing the corporate ladder, high technology, mass marketing, or mergers. To survive here meant manual labor, getting your hands dirty, and working long hours at everything. So many people and businesses had tried and failed, come and gone, but this Vickers bunch had carved a living out of these Rockies with guts and hard work.

Throughout the years, Perk had mined for lead and ore, blasted and built new roads along steep rock cliffs, ran a bulldozer, organized elk and deer hunts, herded cattle and sheep, cut wood, and kept figuring new ways to make money to support the ranch. Emma Jean took care of stressed-out tourists who needed to relax, mothered their children, cleaned log cabins, cooked, and worked in the ranch office. Whatever needed to be done—and there was always something—Buckshot did it even when it was dangerous.

One summer day she was working in the ranch house office when something unusual happened.

Three men drove in and parked on the side of the ranch house office. The driver left his car running, got out, and walked under the elk antlers hanging over the ranch house door and up to the old wooden counter in the office. Emma Jean was the only one there. The man said he needed a place to stay. He and his friends were tired. It was early in the afternoon and Emma Jean explained to him the only cabin she could rent wasn't ready for tourists. It had not been cleaned yet.

"I am not a naive person, and I did not see anything unusual about the man that came in," she said. "You never judge a book by its cover." Emma Jean had taken care of customers for years and years and had learned not to make snap judgments. Besides, most of the people who traveled this far off the beaten path were families on vacation and retired couples who wanted to fish, ride horses, or take jeep trips across the mountains. But the stranger would not be put off and insisted Emma Jean rent him a cabin, dirty or not.

"Just get your maid to make the beds. That's all we're interested in," he said. He told Emma Jean he and his friends would sit in the cabin and wait while the beds were being changed.

On that day, a fifty-year-old woman was helping Emma Jean do maid work, but this woman refused to clean the cabin alone with three men watching her, so Emma Jean said she would go and help change the linens.

"I'll go get my car and show you to your cabin," Emma Jean told the man politely.

"Oh, no. You can get in the car with us," he offered.

Emma Jean was not suspicious but when she crawled in the front of the man's car, she glanced under the dashboard. It was lined with guns.

"Do you have a doctor here in Lake City?" the man asked.

"No, we do not."

"Well," he said, "we got a little powder burn back there."

Emma Jean kept quiet as she rode in the car with the three men, down the gravel lane, across the river and over to their cabin.

"After I saw the guns," she said, "I didn't let on that I didn't see a row of guns under the dashboard everyday."

For the next few days, the three men took shifts, keeping one man outside on the cabin porch all the time to watch. Then they disappeared. She never knew who they really were or what they had done. But for sure, they were running from the law.

"Not any big crimes I guess, probably robbing or something," she mumbled. "Not like the man in the black car who came through."

Emma Jean was better than a mystery novel as she quietly hinted about another story from her secluded life here at the top of the world. She paused, making my curiosity shoot even higher. She lingered over her words and stuttered a little between short throaty laughs. I wanted her to hurry up and tell me. She had a way of making me hang on every word. "I guess this is kind of interesting," she looked down and began the story. Another time when she was working in the ranch house office, a man drove up in a fancy black car and said he'd like to rent a cabin for a few days. He was very well dressed and immaculate. He told her he wanted to get away from business pressures, not be bothered, and just have a leisurely vacation. He owned a fleet of trucks and ran a truck line from Oklahoma to Florida. He paid his cabin rent with one of several credit cards because he didn't like to carry cash.

"I happen to have an electric percolator in the car, and I'd like to give it to you," he said to Emma Jean. She didn't think too much about such a gesture. Maybe the coffee pot was in his way, and he needed to leave it somewhere. Yes, she would take the percolator and appreciated it very much.

"Oh," he said, "I have something else if you'd like to have it—a camera. It takes colored pictures as well as black and white."

Her sharp blue eyes stopped. Emma Jean was basically a trusting person but this sounded strange to her, and she told the man she would have to talk to her husband before accepting the camera.

"Ah, colored pictures," Emma Jean chuckled to herself. "We're talking about this modern age and cameras had been taking colored pictures for a number of years before this man appeared."

The well-dressed man went to his cabin and nothing more was said. Early the next morning he came back to the ranch house office and met Perk and their children, Peggy, Patsy, and Larry, and a couple of the children's cousins. All of the children were quite young at the time, and the man seemed to enjoy them. He was friendly and liked having kids around. Later on the man had to drive his fancy black car into Lake City for mechanical repairs and asked if the children wanted to go. Perk was gone on the bulldozer and Emma Jean still didn't think much about this man. All the youngsters were fascinated with the buttons and gadgets inside his big new car, and they pleaded to go. Off they went to town and returned late in the afternoon.

On the third day, the well-dressed man asked to take all the children on a horseback ride. This time to Crystal Lake, but Emma Jean was beginning to feel uneasy. So was Perk. They made an excuse about one of the children having a cold.

"Something was unusual, but we never let on," Emma Jean remembered. "Thank God, we didn't say 'Boo!' "

Several weeks passed and Emma Jean had forgotten about the man in the black car. After a few days, he had checked out early one morning leaving behind the percolator and camera. Emma Jean was hanging sheets on the clothesline when the telephone call came.

"Are you 'Im-ma' Jean Vickers?" the voice asked.

"I am 'Em-ma' Jean Vickers," she answered.

"Did you accept a percolator and camera from a man a few weeks ago?"

"Ye-e-es?" she answered somewhat puzzled.

"Are you in the habit of accepting gifts from strangers?" the man's voice on the other end of the phone was accusatory and belittling. Emma Jean felt like two cents.

"Ah . . . Mrs. Vickers . . . I must tell you." The voice was careful and continued slowly, "The authorities have just caught this man. He is one of the ten most wanted men in the United States."

Emma Jean was speechless when she heard this well-dressed man who had driven her children to Lake City had escaped from prison, robbed two women on the desert, stolen their car and credit cards, murdered a few people, and more.

"Mrs. Vickers, you did one good thing."

"W-What was that?" she stuttered.

"If he had ever thought you were suspicious of him, he would have shot you on the spot."

❧ ❧ ❧

The Silver Street Saloon was crowded with burly mountain men wearing heavy boots that pounded down on the wood-planked floor. Rough miners with crusty hands and cowboys in wide brimmed hats came through the double door. A bright afternoon sun followed the men inside until they closed the door. A long bar was full of working men leaning over bottles of Colorado beer peeking above their drinks at the mirrored wall behind the counter. Several hometown women, who were the wives or girlfriends of the men, were scattered around the saloon. Four young men were playing pool under a dim bulb hanging down from the ceiling, and six or eight men were huddled under cigar and cigarette smoke in a back corner playing cards. No one admitted if they were gambling.

Country and western music echoed through loudspeakers from an outdated juke box. The sounds of steel guitars, fiddles, and pain-soaked voices made me feel like I was back in Nashville. I had no idea a saloon in the middle of the mountains would be packed at 5:00 P.M. It seemed the place to be, and everyone seemed to know each other. Since most businesses were closed or too slow to make money, and no tourists were around before June, and the hour being at the close of the day, half of the town gathered to talk, and there was laughter, hand shaking, back slapping, and hugging going on between everybody. In Europe, local people visited at a neighborhood pub, but here in Lake City, Colorado, it was the saloon.

Seven of us women were laughing around a crude wooden table next to the wall. Emma Jean had invited Betsy and some of her lady friends to join us for an afternoon pow wow. Behind me was a pot bellied, coal-burning stove and over my head hanging on the wall was a tattered American Flag from the 1800s. This saloon was not a dance disco of neon lights and flashing colors. Here, the walls and atmosphere reflected western life, real and earthy. Around the saloon hung elk horns, horse shoes, a dart board, and deer heads. But what fascinated me most of all were the hundreds of single dollar bills tacked behind the bar all the way to the ceiling. I had never seen anything like that before. Each bill had a name written on it and when I looked closer, there were ten-dollar and twenty-dollar bills too. Why?

"What can I get you girls?" the waitress in boots and blue jeans asked with a friendly smile. She knew everyone at the table except me but that didn't stop me from asking about the bills on the wall.

"Part superstition and mostly tradition," she said. "Old miners would sign their names on the bills so they'd be sure to have money left to buy a drink after they played poker. And some did it for good luck—thinkin' they'd be back and not get killed in the mines."

Just then, Emma Jean's nine-year-old grandson, Garrett, ran through the saloon doors with a big grin on his face. He was out of breath and all excited. Behind him was his grandfather, Perk.

"Pop tipped me!" Garrett shouted. He held up a handful of dollar bills. Garrett had been helping Perk work on the ranch, and his grandfather had given him some money. With a short hug for Emma Jean, Garrett dashed back outside and down to the park to play with some boys. Perk headed to the back table of men playing cards. Perk had a fat cigar in the corner of his mouth and a wide smile on his face. As much as Emma Jean loved to play bridge, Perk loved to play poker.

I lifted my eyebrows. Like a scene from a silent movie, the saloon doors opened, and there stood Tea Black, the miner from Creede, a mining town just over the Continental Divide. For a second, he stood in the doorway outlined in the setting sunlight. He was probably in his late thirties or early forties, medium height, and muscular in build. He strolled to the bar in pointed boots, worn jeans, black leather vest, and giant black cowboy hat. His boots didn't pound on the wooden floor but clicked instead. He had an angular face and full black beard. My first impression of him was that he looked like a cowboy pirate. I nudged Emma Jean.

"These people fascinate me," I whispered in her ear looking around the saloon.

"They're just what they are," Emma Jean commented with a wise nod. "They don't pretend to be anything except what they are."

"You've seen all kinds, haven't you?"

Emma Jean shook her head up and down. "Oh my, yes," she hummed. "I haven't missed anything living here. I've seen people from all walks of life and had great opportunities to meet every kind."

Emma Jean pushed her chair back and walked over to the waitress who was heading toward our table with a tray full of cokes, beer, and wine for all the women.

"Since I invited you ladies, may I?" Emma Jean asked, then handed a twenty-dollar bill to the waitress to pay for the drinks.

Betsy from the clothing store was sitting next to me. She was an attractive, peppy, middle-aged woman with reddish-brown hair, an infectious laugh, big brown eyes, and had known Emma Jean since the early sixties when she started vacationing in Lake City. Their friendship went way back. While Emma Jean was away from the table, Betsy put her arm on the back of my chair and gave me one of those squared-off, show-down looks. For all of

Emma Jean's modesty, Betsy was a fireball. Betsy pointed over her shoulder at Emma Jean who had her back to us.

"That woman pioneered these hills," Betsy declared.

"Why do you say that?"

"Well, my Lord, she came before there was running water, or electricity, or paved roads, or anything."

"Emma Jean fascinates me," I said.

"I adore her!" Betsy cried. Her big brown eyes turned mellow, and the tone in her spirited voice softened. With all the laughter and music in the saloon, Betsy had to talk into my ear for me to hear. "She never finds fault with any person." Betsy took a swallow of her drink and leaned back on her chair with a proud air. I was surprised when she told me her feelings.

"Just talking about her makes me want to cry," Betsy looked away.

Betsy had known Emma Jean twenty-eight years. Maybe she could tell me why Emma Jean would choose to spend her life in the middle of fourteen thousand-foot mountains. Emma Jean had worked hard and had done without more than most women. How many women, young or old, would deny themselves bathrooms, running water, electricity, handy shopping, everyday comforts and conveniences without some good reason? How many women with her potential for a career in the business world would have chosen to wash sheets and scrub floors? In this "me-first" world, people felt they deserved the best—more money, better jobs, faster advancement, quicker returns, more, more, more. This old idea of selflessness and sacrifice was as lost as the gold in these hills.

It all came into focus when Betsy said, "Emma Jean has good stuff inside, and I don't think for one moment she thought she was sacrificing anything to come here— not at all!" Betsy's voice raised and her eyes were angry.

"No! No! No! She loved Perk so much she'd do any-thing. For her family to be happy, that made her happy. It had nothing to do with sacrifice! It had to do with love."

Like a magnet, Betsy drew me closer. She ignored all the other ladies at the table and, fortunately, they were talking among themselves. Betsy leaned into my face. The crowd in the saloon, the country music, the men at the bar, the noise, the outbursts of laughter, everything faded. Across the room, Emma Jean was busy listening to a tired ranch hand called Gary.

"Whatever she does is not to benefit herself. It's be-cause she loves whoever she's doing that for," Betsy said glancing over her shoulder at Emma Jean. "She has love from the top of her head to the tips of her toes and all the way around."

I didn't know what was next, but I could see Betsy was swelling up and ready to explode. Betsy slammed her glass down on the old table and looked up to the ceiling in the saloon. Her voice cracked with memories and feelings that I knew nothing about. "God Almighty!" Betsy wiped some runaway tears from her face and looked around to see if anyone was watching. Right then, I saw how deep the ad-miration and friendship was between these two women. Betsy looked over at Emma Jean and shook her head back and forth and swallowed the lump in her throat.

"God Almighty," she sighed, "what a woman!"

ða ða ða

The next day I had to begin the long journey out of these skyscraper mountains back home to the low and rolling hills of Tennessee and to Rebekah, Jed, and Luke. I missed my three children.

Emma Jean and I were in the ranch house office. She had some paperwork and reservations to check on, and I needed to telephone my children to tell them when I would be home. When I heard Rebekah on the other end of the line, the thousands of miles between us and the two different worlds vanished. Rebekah was talking nonstop in her ten-year-old style, telling me what pranks Jed and Luke were doing, how they were climbing trees and finding imaginary dinosaurs behind bushes while she had made-up a new dance routine with her fifth grade girlfriends at school, and one of her best friends' parents got a new car. It was a Jaguar.

A pang of guilt hit me as I listened to my daughter. I longed to share what I had seen and learned about life in these San Juans. I wished there was some way I could pick up all I knew and had observed from this quiet, self-denying woman known as Buckshot and give it to my little girl. There were sixty years of time and values between Rebekah and Emma Jean—as far as the east is from the west. But somehow, I had to stand in the gap and bridge the distance. I took a deep breath.

Just as I was about to hang up, I heard music coming from the other room—twangy piano notes. Then with the smoothness of silk, the notes turned into beautiful harmony. The sounds were classical, like Beethoven. Hurridly, I smacked a kiss over the phone to the kids and told them goodbye. Then I quietly made my way to the doorway and peeked around the corner.

There she sat. Buckshot was playing the piano. It was an old upright piano with enough cobwebs and dust to fill a bucket. It sat in the corner of the ranch house behind a horse saddle. A deer head hung on the wall over the old piano with a water canteen dangling from one of the antlers. There in her porcupine earrings, furlined boots, and blue jeans, Emma Jean sat on an old twirl-top stool, with her skillful hands floating across the keyboard. Some of the notes were dead, but enough keys worked to make the melody sound whole. She didn't know I was watching because she had her head turned upward and was looking out the window toward the mountains and the Continental Divide.

Without any effort, or glancing down at the keys, her fingers moved into a familiar tune. It was rich and warm and tugged at my memory. I caught my breath when I realized what she was playing.

> . . . when I in awesome wonder,
> Consider all the worlds Thy Hands have made.
> I see the stars, I hear the rolling thunder,
> Thy pow'r thro'out the universe displayed. . . .
>
> When I look down from lofty mountain
> grandeur,
> And hear the brook and feel the gentle
> breeze . . .
>
> Then sings my soul, my Savior God to Thee
> How Great Thou Art! . . .
> How Great Thou Art!

It was a private and tender moment, better than a church service, as Emma Jean's sweet music filled the ranch house and drifted out the front door, past the horse corral and hay barn and evaporated into the mountains. I felt like I was standing on holy ground. Hidden from the world like an uncut diamond, I had only scratched the surface of this woman. She was deeper than I would ever know.

Suddenly, she turned and saw me standing there. Immediately she stopped, and her shyness returned.

Quietly I said, "I didn't know you could play so beautifully."

"Ah-h-h, yes, I'm such an accomplished pianist," she blushed. "Anything in the key of C . . . I've got it."

FRIED PIES FROM BUCKSHOT

Oh mercy! . . . Let me think. . . . Get some Hungry Jack Biscuits, I believe there's ten in a can, and whatever dried fruit you like. I prefer apricots. Just cook the apricots on the stove with water. It doesn't take an awful long time, and then when they have boiled down and are tender enough, just dump in enough sugar. Taste it.

You know what a fruit pie looks like? The biscuit is round so roll it out, put the dried fruit inside and fold it over. Pinch around the edge with a fork. Ummmm . . . you know, like you do with a pie crust. Then get your Crisco oil out and get your pan ready. You don't need a real deep pan. Pour about a half inch oil. Get those pies ready before youstart cooking. You don't have time to do the pies and cook at the same time.

Get all ten pies ready to go, cook about three at a time. I used to use the old iron skillet, but I like an electric skillet better. Ummm . . . I think about 350 degrees.

You just kind of have to watch them. I'm not real sure how long—until they're brown. Take them out, put on a paper towel so the grease will drain. Put the next batch in.

They don't need any ice cream or anything else to my way of thinking. Serve them with coffee. Yes, that's fine. They really don't go too well with wine.

 za za za

Chapter Three

A TEXAS RUBY

THE AMERICAN AIRLINER 727 jet roared off the runway, lifting the plane load of us up and out of the misting rain and stormy morning at the International Airport in Nashville, Tennessee. My seat belt was buckled, carry-on bags stored in the overhead compartment, and my purse was tucked under the seat. Whew! I felt relieved. There were doubts whether I'd make this 6:30 A.M. flight. It was bad enough to hear the alarm clock scream at 4:30 A.M. and wake me in time to splash on my makeup, throw on my blue jeans and sweat shirt, load the car, drive from home in Nashville to the airport, get parked. All in time to catch this early flight, but then to have to fly in such bad weather made me nervous and uneasy. Pushing through the thick sky and choppy air, higher and higher the plane climbed; I slowly began to relax. The muscles in my body began to un-tighten.

There was a medium-sized man in his mid-forties, with brown hair and hints of gray, wearing blue jeans, cowboy boots, and a short leather jacket sitting next to me reading *The Tennessean*, the Nashville morning newspaper. He was absorbed in the sports page and didn't notice me looking over his arm to see if he was finished with the front page. Although he wore western gear, he didn't look like a rough cowboy because his hands were smooth and appeared soft. I wondered what he did for a living but was more interested in reading the newpaper whenever he finished. I planned to ask to read it, but not now. We were only minutes out of Nashville.

The plane was full of sleepy passengers. As the turbulent atmosphere became calmer, everyone seemed to settle down for an even flight to Dallas, Texas. It would take at least two hours. Since it wouldn't be long before light-footed flight attendants would start serving coffee and breakfast, I needed more sleep—even thirty minutes would help. My eyes were drooping as I laid back on the head cushion and thought about Texas and my destination. I felt tired and sleepy, but it wasn't hard to think back. It had been almost ten years since I had seen the Great Plains of west Texas, or been back to the wild and wooly country of diamondback rattlesnakes, hungry coyotes, and long horned cattle—back to the hot winds, powdery red dirt, zippy road runners, and wide open spaces. My half awake mind was remembering the jagged canyons, cracked earth, scrubby dry grass, delicate bluebonnets, pumping oil wells, tumbleweed, windmills, and all the friendly people I knew. I had known the land and the people well. But a lot had happened over a decade. Happy and not-so-happy changes had taken place in my life, and I wondered what changes I'd find on this return trip. What had the passing of time done there?

I was going back to see my rancher friends, Ruby and Homer Martin, who lived about 250 miles west of Fort Worth where they raised wheat and cattle. We had met back in 1977, the year I spent walking across their big, hot state of Texas, sweating across America on foot from New Orleans to Oregon and writing an article for *National*

Geographic Magazine. Texas and The Martin Ranch were on the way west.

For several days and nights in 1977, I had rested on their ranch and had eaten Ruby's home cooking and spent memorable hours sitting and talking to Ruby. One particular night after a violent thunderstorm swept across their ranch, I remember we sat on their front porch, and she told me stories from her early years. Ruby told me about life in the "old days" and while she talked, crickets sang, and the sweet smell of damp sagebrush filled the night. Earthy smells came out as the black Texas sky filled up with blinking stars, and coyotes yelped far off. It felt like I was in a movie set listening to her western stories. That night on their porch, Texas and this woman called Ruby both seemed bigger than life.

As the jet plane roared toward Dallas, Ruby was the reason I felt pulled back. *Yes . . . I needed to see this woman again, this woman I once knew.* With that thought, I decided to fade into oblivion and make up for the 4:30 A.M. alarm clock. I was almost asleep.

"Excuse me, ma'am. Would you like a vegetable omelet or pancakes?" the attendant asked.

The man next to me with the soft hands and newspaper reached for his breakfast tray carefully so as not to disturb me. With sleepy eyes, I pulled myself up, yawned, and decided on pancakes. I'd sleep after breakfast. A cup of juice and hot coffee would feel good.

"May I read your newspaper?" I asked since the paper was folded in his lap.

He smiled, "Sure," then handed it to me. He seemed like a nice man. I wondered again what he did for a living. While I rubbed butter on pancakes and fumbled with the newspaper, he began talking to a long-haired man sitting across the aisle. They were discussing Nashville, country music, songs, studio bands, and concerts. It was hard for me not to overhear bits of their conversation although I kept eating and reading the paper.

"Thank you for sending me a Christmas card. Most guys in your position don't do things like that," said the long-haired man across the aisle. He was talking to the man next to me.

My sleep-hungry eyes opened wide and curiosity about the man next to me started building by the second. What *did* he do? He looked like an average guy, very normal, and certainly no one I had ever seen. Before I ate all my breakfast, I found myself searching for a way to talk to him. I took another bite and thought hard. How could I find out what this man did for a living without embarassing myself or intruding?

"You have business in Nashville?" I finally asked.

"Yes, Ma'am."

"The weather sure was bad this morning. I don't like to fly when it's stormy and bad."

"I don't either." His voice was mellow.

"You live in Nashville?"

"San Antonio," he answered. Either he was bashful, bored, didn't want to talk, or secretive, but there was some reason he was holding back. His reticence only made me more curious.

"You come to Nashville often?"

"Quite a bit, but I do a lot of traveling," he answered modestly.

"Oh!" I said with a clip. "What do you do?"

"Well," he said quietly, "I'm a singer." His voice was almost a whisper.

"You are?" I exclaimed. My shock must have shown because he smiled and nodded calmly. I felt like I was going to explode if he didn't tell me more.

"Are you in country music?" I asked.

He nodded. He wasn't wearing sequins, flashy clothes. There was no jewelry, no earring in his ear, no bushy, crinkled hair, nothing to make him stand out in a crowd. His face was smooth with very few lines. *He's probably getting started in the music business and sings backup for somebody famous*, I thought.

"Do you sing honky-tonk, bluegrass, or what?" I asked out of ignorance. Although I had recently moved to Nashville, I was not familiar with the ins-and-outs of country music.

"More middle of the road." He crossed his legs and folded his hands. He looked at me, and I thought I saw sympathy on his face. There was a long pause and a kind smile.

"I've had thirty-five songs in the top ten," he said.

"Wha-a-t?" I gulped. My voice could be heard all over the plane. "Who are you?" I cried.

In a low hush, he told me his name.

I had never heard of him and was at a loss, but my honesty and naiveté about country music stars made him friendly. For the next hour and a half, until we landed in Dallas, we talked nonstop about his hit records, singing tours all over the world, his wife and three children, his cattle ranch, Nashville, and the country music industry.

It seemed uncanny for me to be ushered back to Texas by a man born and raised outside San Antonio and who was also a very famous country and western singer. When I told him about going back to see Ruby, returning after so many years, his steadfast eyes told me he understood. The love of Texas was in his soul and in his hit songs, too.

ಜ ಜ ಜ

The narrow road up to Ruby and Homer's small ranch house was usually hard packed dirt, but today it was muddy, full of deep ruts, and looked clay red because of a recent heavy rain. Their grey-shingled ranch house looked like I remembered it except there was a new chimney on one end, decorated with the big letter "M" for Martin. The house sat like a beacon in the middle of flat, wide-open fields. There were no trees or shrubs in the front yard. Long rows of wheat with tiny green shoots surrounded their house and bordered the driveway and yard. Except for their house and outbuildings, there was nothing on the horizon but a lonely windmill off in the distance and an old vacant house way down the straight country road.

In the driveway sat Homer's grey, 1976 Dodge pickup truck. *My goodness, he still has it.* It was a new truck back when I was here. There was a late model van sitting beside the pickup truck, and I wondered who else was visiting. Looking across the ranch, I wondered if they still had their dog, Benji.

When I stopped my car next to the pickup truck, suddenly the screen door flew open, and both Ruby and Homer ran out across the cement porch and down the steps to meet me. Their arms were stretched open, and faces lit up with smiles as wide as their wheat fields. They grabbed and hugged me and our laughter rang out across the openness. Homer was a tall Texan, lean and muscular for a man in his mid-seventies, and he held his trusty cowboy hat in one hand while he squeezed me tight.

"Oh, it sure is good to see you!" he grinned, showing a mouthful of teeth. His blue eyes glittered.

"We just been so excited," Ruby sang, with her arm around my waist. "Come on in."

"You two haven't changed a bit. You both look great!" I cheered.

"Law, girl . . . We jus' keep-a-goin'," Ruby giggled.

"Where's Benji?" I asked as we walked toward the porch steps.

"Well, Barbara," Ruby stopped and sighed. Ruby and Homer never had any children, so I knew how special this little dog was to them. Ruby pointed toward the road. "One night I looked up at the north side of the sidewalk, and there he was—layin' out there, and when Homer went to him, Benji didn't whine or nothin' . . . just kinda wiggled his tail and never said a word and died." Ruby shook her head with a renewed sadness. "He was fifteen years old." I looked over at Homer who stood on the porch, shaking his head and twiddling his fingers against his cowboy hat. That little dog had been like a family member. Ruby said, "After that, Homer told me, 'We're not ever gonna have another dog. Never gonna have another one!' " Ruby looked over at Homer standing on the porch, and then she grinned, "So, we went down to Wichita Falls, down to the pet shop, an' there was a dog there jus' exactly like ol' Benji. So Homer wanted to buy it, but I told him that's not Benji and don't expect it to be!" Ruby looked over at Homer and chuckled. "Well sir, Homer went up there and ask 'em about the dog. They wanted 350 dollars fer it!"

Homer kicked his cowboy boots on the cement steps and let out a gutsy laugh, "Sure enough, it wasn't Benji! And I backed out purty quick!"

With our arms locked around each other, Ruby escorted me inside her home. When the screendoor closed behind us, it felt as if it were 1977 again, except for the new fireplace that took up one wall on the end of the front room. It was light tan brick with black mortar and a knee-high hearth where you could sit and warm your back against the fire. Since that brick wall faced the oncoming winter winds, I knew it fought off the cold northers that whipped across the plains. The mantel over the fireplace was loaded with Texas treasures. There was a brass long-horned bull, a novelty plate, an empty wine bottle, trinkets, and an American flag hanging on one side of the mantel and the Texas state flag hanging on the other.

Their console television sat in the corner beside the fireplace with a small lamp on top. I remembered that lamp. It was a wagon wheel lamp, and the shade was off-white with a picture of a Hereford bull on it. There was a stack of magazines and farm journals on the floor beside the sofa with one of Homer's cowboy hats resting on top of the pile. Two recliner chairs faced the fireplace and television and both had handmade afghans thrown across them. One was crocheted in cream-colored yarn with chocolate brown trim and the other was green, orange, and white. Of course, I knew Ruby had made them.

The same linoleum covered the floor. It was a light vinyl that looked like spotted pebbles. There were several area carpet rugs scattered on the floor. The chrome dinner table with four metal folding chairs sat in the same spot, against the kitchen wall on one side and a chest freezer on the other side. Over the table hung a picture of Jesus and the twelve disciples eating The Last Supper. Next to the Jesus picture hung a wooden plaque which read, "Live As Though Every Day Was Your Last—And Someday You Will Be Right."

Another sign hung on the back of the front door. It was a shiny and simple pie pan with the design of a valentine heart in the middle. Instead of the heart being drawn, it had been stamped out with tiny nail holes and inside the heart was the word, *Welcome* in capital letters. I knew that welcome sign was for real in this house.

"We know worlds of people, an' we love people . . . jus' different ones," Ruby said. "I guess I'm like my dad cause I never met a stranger, and if Dad went to town and found someone that didn't have no place to stay, he brought 'em home." She smiled with her narrow blue eyes that weren't fooled by appearances, fast talk, or big dollars. I knew this was true because my appearance as a backpacker walking across America in 1977 didn't fool or frighten her. Her home was open to me back when I had nothing except the clothes on my back.

After I had glanced around the small and homey den and kitchen area, I turned to take a good look at Ruby as she stood like the tall, 5′ 8″ Texas woman I remembered, resting her current 140 pounds on one leg with the other leg slightly bent at the knee and pointed outward. She was wearing a royal blue blouse, comfortable dark slacks, and leather loafers. She reminded me of a statue, proud and solid all the way through. Her shoulders were straight across and her head held high. Her jaw line was square and her face still strong and spirited. She wore a blush of pink lipstick that made her smile seem mighty tender. Her short grey hair was shiny and stylish and still naturally curly.

She fidgeted with the top of her hair. "Ever' body else is wearin' ther hair all frizzed-up on ther head, so I decided I would too."

We both laughed, and then Ruby locked her square jaw and said matter-of-factly, "I'll be seventy-nine in March."

"What are you a tellin' yer age for?" Homer quipped, good naturedly.

"Cause I want to," she said walking past him. Ruby shot an electric look in Homer's direction. She poked, "I don't let Homer boss me around!"

"Aw-w-w, why not?" I asked.

"Shoot, girl! That's the wrong thing to do," she answered, walking away and into the kitchen with a frisky almost seventy-nine-year-old step. It felt good to be with these two again.

"We're gonna eat lunch soon, but y'all want orange juice, grape juice, apple juice or coffee now?" Ruby asked from around the corner. "I've got some ham on a cookin', some potatoes, some black-eyed peas. There's a fruit salad made, and I'll make us a pan of biscuits." Yep! I was back in Texas. The best way to entertain a guest in these parts was to fatten 'em up (like cattle) until they couldn't move.

Suddenly, Homer jumped like he'd seen a rattlesnake and when his cowboy boots hit the floor, he began to pull out several wooden crafts from the next room. He handed me wooden toys, mouse traps, salt and pepper holders, a miniature rocking chair, a plaque with the name *Jesus* camouflaged in the design, and a recipe holder that said, "I'm not afraid to face tomorrow."

"I've made a world of these things," Homer said with a handsome and proud smile. His full head of grey hair was cut the same as when he was a Navy man back in 1942.

"So this is what you've been doing since you retired?" I asked. Homer had worked for the Santa Rosa Telephone Company until 1981 when he retired. Now, he and Ruby traveled to different parts of the United States to attend board meetings. Homer was a board member for the National Telephone Cooperative of America and had served the past ten years.

Ruby was walking back and forth from the kitchen setting bowls of steaming food on the chrome table, pouring lemonade, and adding dishes of relish, olives, and butter. She didn't want me to help her yet.

"Some folks say he oughta sell his crafts. Well, why? He enjoys makin' and givin' 'em away, so . . . What else? We don't have nobody to leave 'em to," Ruby said. She looked at Homer and me out of the corner of her eyes. "I'm fixin' to take up these potatoes, so you outlaws come on."

Sure enough, no sooner had I pulled my metal chair under the small table, and Homer had said "Amen" from blessing the supper, than at the same time, they both handed me bowls of food.

"Here, hep yerself," Ruby said. "These aren't them city potatoes." My plate was filling up fast.

"Oh, I've had a time, I'll tell ya," Homer sighed with a somber tone.

Ruby explained, "That doctor that took out Homer's last kidney stone said it was the only one he'd ever seen that large. It was like a strawberry with burrs all over it." She dipped black-eyed peas on her plate. "He's got two of 'em now. Bless his heart, he's dreadin' this next time. He's supposed to go in a couple weeks to get it done," she said, handing me the platter of biscuits.

"It's this new laser business. They're gonna put me to sleep, and I jus' don't think I can be put to sleep anymore," he said.

"Yeah, ya can. Go ahead and say yer gonna be all right," Ruby told Homer. "Just don't give up, yer gonna be all right."

"Do you have to watch what you eat?" I asked with concern.

"You bet. Anything I put in my mouth that tastes good, I have to spit it out!" he laughed. His easy-going smile returned. Ruby groaned, "Oh-h-h, we don't pay that much attention, but we did take him off dairy products."

"Well sir, that thang there," Homer pointed toward Ruby. "If I had part of her health, I'd be all right." Before she could swallow her mouth full of food and make a comment, Homer added, "Not one time has she been in the hospital in her life!"

"Tell me your secret," I asked.

"There ain't but one thing the matter with her. She's just too mean to get sick," Homer said.

Ruby laughed under her breath. "Yeah, but you won't trade me off!" she countered. "We'll be married fifty-seven years on June 7th."

Homer looked at me and shook his head, "Ain't that a long time to live with one woman?"

☙ ☙ ☙

We talked a long time over lunch, catching up on news of family and friends from Texas and Tennessee and all that was happening with my three children, Rebekah, Jed, and Luke. Over the years, we had stayed in close touch, and my children were special to them. After finishing the last sip of coffee and with full stomachs, we pushed ourselves away from the table and began clearing the dishes. I was ready to wash the plates in the kitchen sink when Ruby told me to stop.

"Have to heat water to wash dishes and bathe," she said as she put a big kettle of water on the electric stove to heat. Their hot water heater had been broken over a month.

"Our house needs a lot of work done on it, but ya can't get anybody to do it cause we live sa far out," Ruby said. Ruby and Homer had built this three-room ranch house in 1947 and had lived here since. "We're talkin about buyin' another place." Ruby cleared her throat a couple of times to hide her feelings. Quietly, she added, "We know sooner or later we're gonna have to move in closer."

Looking out Ruby's one kitchen window, there lay 193 acres that had been in the Martin family since 1908. It was just dirt. But, it surrounded their house and had been Ruby and Homer's lifeline all these years. They had plowed it, planted cotton, wheat, and milo on it, hoed it, watched cattle graze on it, harvested crops on it, raised chickens and hogs on it, and had stood on its flat surface many nights, looking back and forth across the horizon for signs of tornados or a red haze of prairie fire. The dust from these fields had been wiped off Ruby's furniture for nearly fifty-seven years. And she'd scrubbed many dresses and work clothes on a washboard, pounding and brushing out the dirt from this land that had been home.

"But this house is better than that ol' shack out yonder," she said pointing toward the driveway. "We lived in it over a year after we married in '33."

She handed me empty glasses from the table and motioned for me to dump the remaining ice cubes in the sink while she put lids on the pickles and butter and set them back in the refrigerator. "That shack only had one room and there was no plumbin' and no runnin' water. We got our water out of a cistern. So, shoot, girl! Not havin' hot runnin' water is nothin' to me," Ruby chuckled. The big kettle of water on the electric stove started to whistle.

"Why, I've learned how to make do from the time I was four years old when we was a comin' to Texas in a covered wagon," Ruby declared, "back in 1915." Once more, I shook my head in disbelief because here was a square-shootin', true-grit, true-to-life pioneer woman, standing and talking to me right out of the pages of American history while we washed dishes together in her Texas kitchen.

"There was twelve of us in my family and we had three covered wagons. I rode on a different wagon each day. My dad and older brothers drove the wagons from Durant, Oklahoma to Ford City, Texas." She smiled. "An' when we got to Ford City, we lived in tents from December til February."

I was spellbound as I stood and leaned against the kitchen counter while she told me how their family survived through that bitter cold winter.

"Oh, girl, it wasn't any problem to stay warm. Ya know when yer young and active and yer used to it, it doesn't hurt ya. Where, now, we're used to all the comforts in the world," she exclaimed. Ruby handed me a knife to put in the drawer, then she pointed toward a stack of saucers. I wasn't paying attention to what she wanted me to do because my imagination was focused on her covered wagon story.

"There's a cuptowel," she motioned.

"What am I supposed to do?"

"Law, girl, didn't your mother ever teach you anything?" she said. "Wipe 'em off." Drying dishes was a million miles away from my thoughts as I envisioned Ruby and her large family traveling the dusty trails to Texas in a covered wagon—pioneers in search of a better life, slapping the rear ends of livestock to keep them moving, horses and wagons, rugged men in boots and wide brimmed hats, gutsy women in gingham dresses and bonnets, squeaky axles and wheels, camping along the creek banks, rumpled and carefree kids playing, and more. Ruby . . . Ruby. She had lived it! This woman I was helping in her kitchen had bridged history in a way no one else I knew had done. Not only had she come to Texas in a covered wagon, before paved roads, fast cars, telephones, electricity, and televisions, but she had also carved a life out of this Texas dirt and had loved and lived with the same man for fifty-seven years.

"Yep, we brought mattresses and clothes, a wood stove, and iron bedsteads in the wagons and when we got to

Ford City, we put up the stove and beds in the tents. A tent, when it's fixed right, it's pretty warm," she shrugged her shoulders.

I used the cuptowel to wipe the dishes while Ruby puttered around stacking pans and bowls in the cupboards. "My dad leased some land and then bought a little farm in Crowell where I went to school. I finished the eighth grade there, from Beaver School, an' then decided I wanted to get out on my own."

"You left home? After the eighth grade?" I was shocked.

"Barely fifteen," she grinned. "My folks didn't like me takin' off so young, but they knew if I made up my mind, I was gonna do it anyway. My girlfriend, Lolla Belle and I, we highwayed-it to Lubbock."

"Hitchhiked?"

Ruby couldn't help but laugh at me when she saw my mouth drop open. "Used to, you didn't give it a thought. It wasn't bad. I jus' wanted to see what this old world was tickin' about, but I come back home and got a job as a waitress."

About that time, Homer strolled into the kitchen with a broad grin across his face. While we cleaned up the dishes, he had been sitting in his recliner chair and listening to us talk from the cozy den. He stood tall and his chest swelled out as he clicked his black cowboy boots on the linoleum.

"She come home and discovered the best thing in her life," Homer bragged, pointing toward himself. He was lit up like a Christmas ornament, and I had to restrain myself from giving him an affectionate hug.

"Was it love at first sight?" I teased.

"Well sir," he drawled, "all my mother's people lived up at Crowell where Ruby was, and I just happened over

there one time and I said, 'That's my gal, right there!' "
He pointed at Ruby.

Ruby stacked the last plate in the cabinet, turned toward me and added, "We met in October and married in
June of '33." She wiped her hands, hung the towel, and
cut her eyes over at Homer with a flirty look, "It took me
that long to make up my mind."

Homer leaned over and kissed Ruby on the cheek,
"Watch it now," he said.

Ruby dried her hands for the last time and folded the
cuptowel neatly on the counter top. She locked her fingers together and stood silent for a moment, in her own
thoughts. I stood watching her and wondered if she was
waiting to tell me something. She probably wanted to tell
me more about their courtship or early days of their marriage, or another pioneer story.

Out of the blue, she said, "Oh, my hands are ugly!"

She caught me off guard, and without thinking, I
blurted, "Those are the hands that have picked cotton,
been a waitress, planted gardens, fed cattle, hoed and
chopped weeds . . ." I wished I could quickly remember all
Ruby had done in her life. "Ruby, you have wonderful
hands." They were agile and smooth for the heavy and
hard work she had done over three quarters of a century.
There were no arthritic knots, swollen joints, or scars.
They were strong and helping hands. She still cooked and
carried food to the elderly, quilted, crocheted, and cared
for others.

Caught in a self-conscious moment, Ruby was quick to
change the subject as she walked out of the kitchen and
into the living room motioning for me to follow her. It
was time to sit back in front of the fireplace, rest, and
ponder all we'd talked about since I had arrived and
walked through their front door with the welcome sign

hanging on the back of it. Gladly, I followed and slumped down on the sofa, stretched my legs in front of me and laid back my head. It felt good to relax.

This simple home on the western plains really was like a lighthouse in the middle of a troubled sea. Ruby and Homer's home fires were rare in this fast and throw-away age. Like basking on a hidden island where it was warm and healing and safe, I sat on their sofa, with my eyes half closed.

"Why, I like to have forgot to show ya my quilt," Ruby sang, jarring me fully awake. "I laid it out whar I wouldn't forget." She bounced out of her recliner chair and dashed into her bedroom, then hurried back with her arms stretched high and wide holding a colorful large handmade quilt.

She cheered, "I'm so proud of it."

There before me was a quilt of many colors—reds, greens, yellows, blues, and deep browns, designed blocks of fabric and enough stitches to make a calculator dizzy. "This is the first quilt we did in my group. There's sixteen of us women in the Home Extension Service, and we drawed names to see which one got it, and . . . I got the first one!" she beamed. She draped the handmade quilt with reverence over her easy chair like a royal robe so each block could be seen clearly. Homer watched proudly.

"Look at this right here, the yellow rose of Texas," Ruby said, pointing with pride. She pointed to other details and chattered, "We jus' have more fun, sewin' and talkin' about cannin', how to shop, what will save us money, swappin' coupons, and" she joked, "you know what it is when a bunch o' women get together."

"They get up there and tell what thar husbands done," Homer cracked.

"Or, what they didn't do," Ruby countered. "We quilted one for the crippled children in Abilene and it brought three to four hundred dollars. We started quiltin' in '86 and have been quiltin' since, and we'll draw names until all sixteen of us get a quilt." Ruby was so excited and thrilled over her quilt that she reminded me of a little girl showing off her birthday present.

After we admired the fine needlework and the creative patterns throughout the quilt, Ruby sat down in her easy chair with a fatigued sigh and laid the colorful spread across her lap, almost to her shoulders. Her arms wrapped around it, holding each stitch and each lady friend who had helped make the quilt close to her heart. For all of Ruby's spunk and zesty ways, I could tell she was wearing down and needed to catnap. Even though she didn't look or act it, she wasn't a young woman anymore.

Her eyes were hanging low, and the snug den turned from an excited showplace into a calm stillness as we sat there in front of the low burning fire. There was only the sound of wood burning—a crackle and popping noise coming from the fireplace. Ruby's head began to nod. She fought falling asleep, but Homer was glad to see her sit down and relax as he watched her out of the corner of his eye.

"Homer gets after me and says I can't sit still for five minutes but maybe I can for three minutes before I think of something to do. He'll say, 'Ya lacked two minutes.' "

A tranquil mood fell on the room as we all slipped in and out of drowsy stages of rest. Homer was comfortable in his reclining chair, Ruby was definitely nodding off in her easy chair, and I was half-awake, half-asleep on the couch. My own semi-consciousness made me think I was dreaming when I heard a faint cry, "eo-w, eo-w, eo-w." The western den was shadowy and quiet. Maybe I was imagining things as I took a leisurely sigh and closed my eyes tighter. Then I heard it again, "eo-w, eo-w, eo-w."

I opened one eye and looked over at Homer. "What's that?"

"Cay-ot-e," Homer whispered. "Sounds like a dyin' rabbit when they go ta cryin'."

"They're still around?" I mumbled.

Homer kept his voice low, "You bet, they're around but ever' thing else is gone. Don't see road runners anymore, don't see a jackrabbit but onct ever month. Ya don't never see a skunk either. Them cayotes has got 'em all, I guess." Homer paused and under his breath, he said, "But them wild hogs is taken over now."

Ruby was fast asleep in her chair, so I took a deep breath, groaned a little, shut my eyes once more and faded back into never-never land. I'd ask about those wild hogs later.

ᔆ ᔆ ᔆ

The next day, it was windy and almost like March instead of mid-winter when the three of us headed across a wheat field to look at the ol' shack where Ruby and Homer first lived after they married. The ground was loose and muddy. It was a sunny January day, nippy cold, but a pleasant change from the stormy weather this part of Texas had had a few days earlier.

"This was the first rain we've had since we sowed ar wheat back in September," Ruby told me. She was feeling good, bubbly, quick on her feet, and just as quick with her comments as we walked past Homer's woodworking shop and through one of the wheat fields headed toward the road. Our shoes and Homer's boots sunk in the wet ground. We circled around by the tractor barn that housed Homer's 1950 tractor.

"Runs better now than when I bought it."

We turned and made our way toward the one room shack which stood like a square box, built out of wide plank boards that had weathered from a rich brown wood to an ashen gray. There were big cracks between the boards where the wind and rain and snow could blow through. It had a tin roof on top. The scrubby, ancient building stood alone, surrounded by ironscraps and over-grown weeds, like a memorial to the past.

"Out here in this ol' shack, we ordered our first bunch of baby chickens," Ruby remembered. "At night I'd bring 'em in, and put 'em back in the cartons they was shipped in, and put a lamp down in there to keep 'em warm." Her smile was as fresh as this day's sunshine. "So, we slept with the chickens at night in this shack."

There was not a glimmer of resentment about starting her married life with Homer back in 1933 in this scrappy and primitive hut with a bunch of chirping chickens fifty-seven years ago. Ruby was almost jovial as she told me how they lived here for over a year.

"We had a little oil cookstove, no runnin' water. It had a wood floor, the bathroom outside . . ." her voice trailed off as she stopped and thought back. "We used orange crates for furniture and why, I didn't even have an icebox to keep meat, so whenever we raised our chickens, I'd wring their necks and dress 'em on Saturday evening."

"Yuk!"

Ruby laughed at me when I turned up my nose. "Shoot, girl, that's easier than choppin' ther heads off. Ya jus' take its head in yer hand and give it a swing, an' twist it off." She laughed using her hands to show me how to twist and swing the chicken. "Then ya pick and scald the chicken and turn the burner on the stove and singe off the hair. We'd kill as many as three chickens and started from scratch when company come down here on Sundays after church."

Times had sure changed since '33, I thought. Wringing a chicken's neck and picking and scalding one was a long way from the meat department at Kroger's or popping chicken nuggets in the microwave. We faced the morning sun and walked carefully away from the shack and toward the country road in front of their ranch. The chilly wind was stinging our faces.

"It's a wonder one of these tornados hadn't blown that shack away," Ruby said quietly. Dozens of times over the years, she had heard the deafening roar and watched vicious black funnels rip across the land. "Ya never get over bein' scared of 'em," she said, dodging a muddy hole and a big red ant mound.

We were almost to the road when we passed the old cistern where she had drawn water while living in the shack. It was a deep hole that caught rainwater, and dead shrubs and runaway weeds had grown up all around. The thought of drinking rainwater wasn't too appealing but, back then, there wasn't a public health department or chemical plant to treat drinking water. We stopped long enough to look down inside the reservoir.

"If there was any tadpoles in the water, we'd strain 'em out and pour a little Clorox in thar to kill the bugs," Ruby chuckled.

I was amazed to see how Ruby and Homer had survived such unsanitary and crude living conditions. Today, when most newlyweds start out life together, there would be one or two cars, a modern apartment or condominium with one or two bathrooms, air conditioning, central heat, a kitchen full of modern appliances, and clean desk jobs or the security of a labor union. Looking at this older couple standing on the same land where they had started their lives together, they were both remarkably healthy and spry for their age and all the hardships and inconveniences had not hurt them one bit. They continued to be two of the strongest Americans, in body and spirit, I had seen anywhere across the country.

"We was always healthy," she said. "We jus' always worked hard and was out in the open, in the fresh air, and we ate home-grown vegetables."

Directly across from the cistern were piles of scrap iron, old tools, rusted metal, and junk. Outdated and discarded piles of farm equipment were stacked like islands in the middle of a sea of wheat fields. The brisk, gusty breeze carried a terrible smell across the openness and toward us. Ruby wrinkled her nose.

"Pe-ew!" Ruby said. "Somebody round here run over a polecat." She pulled her coat around her and zipped the front. "Boy! I'm sure glad I wore my coat. That wind's cold." She shivered.

We finally set foot on the empty country road and meandered down the lane away from the old honeymoon shack and ranch.

"It's nice to live out in the country cause if I take a notion to whip Ruby, they can't hear her a hollerin'," Homer chuckled.

My bellows of laughter could be heard a mile down the lonely road all the way to the windmill. There was the crunch of rocks and soft ground under our feet and the whistle of endless wind. The drone of a pickup truck could be heard from far away. We walked side by side, all of us in a good mood and talking about the old days compared to how the world was today—drugs, violence, and crime. How kids have a harder time growing up, and more.

"So hep me, I know'd this boy all his life, and he was a growin' it. I never saw so many F.B.I.'s." She paused, then added, "Over two million dollars worth of stuff the law got."

"And in a little place like this!" Homer chimed in. "That's the thing about it." He shook his head in disbelief.

"Law . . . how many families it broke up here," Ruby said sadly.

"I'll tell ya, it scares me. And, I'll tell ya who I feel sorry fer, it's the kiddos today," Homer said.

"They get a hold of our young people before they know what's happenin'." Ruby stuck her hands in her coat pocket and squared her shoulders with a fury. "It's so hard for young people. All they're faced with is dope and sex!"

"Too much temptation!" Homer added.

Ruby began to tell the story of a young lady she had known for a long time, and they were close friends. One day last year, this young woman telephoned Ruby. "It was on a Friday and she asked if Homer was in the house. I told her he was outside plowin' the garden. Then she said, 'Ruby, I love you.' " Standing in the middle of the muddy road, Ruby took a heavy breath and stopped in her tracks. Her jaw and legs were both locked in place as she eyed me with an unwavering look. The wind whipped around us. Homer walked ahead, surveying the fields that ran alongside the road. Ruby continued, "I could read what the woman was a tryin' to tell me. I could tell she was high on dope right then. She'd talk, and ever little bit, she'd say, 'Ruby, I love you.' And, I told her 'Don't do it.' That was on a Friday, and she took her life on a Sunday night. She was thirty-four . . . left a baby."

Tested and tried Ruby turned away from me and lowered her head. She was silent as she looked across the flat horizon, shielding her eyes from the cold bright sun. Then she reached for a Kleenex in her coat pocket and dabbed her eyes.

"That's what's the matter with the world—drugs and lettin' 'em get by with it."

Out of nowhere, the wind blew a tumbleweed across the road in front of us, and the gust seemed to pick up a piece of the pain inside of Ruby and carry it away, like the tumbleweed, off down the road and out of sight. Ruby held her head high and she shot back.

"We all have hope ever' day, but then somethin' tells ya, 'I don't believe the Good Lord's gonna let it keep goin' on like it is.'" She narrowed her eyes that had seen about every kind of hardship seventy-nine years of living could bring, but the pain in her voice told me she thought living in the world today was even harder. "God's about the only hope, but He can't do anything except weaken the people doin' drugs and sellin' em, and they're gonna have to repent."

Homer was quite a ways ahead of us examining the tiny green growth coming out of the dirt. The wheat wasn't as high as normal because of the long dry spell, but the sprouts from the recent rain were signs of new life and a new crop. He looked back and hollered, "That wheat should be *up* and the cattle grazin' on it." Then he walked further on, checking the washed-out gulleys alongside the road.

Ruby nudged me and grinned. We strolled beside each other, quietly, step in step with nowhere to go and no meetings to attend, no schedule and no time clock to follow. This day was beautiful. My soul felt like it had been blown clean and filled with pure and simple things from the Texas winds and from Ruby, the strong plainswoman. She was as open and dependable as her land, and as unchanging. Her life had not been an easy one from the day she arrived by covered wagon in 1915. And the years had not allowed her to grow soft with ease and luxury, but she was as wise and knowledgeable as any human being I had ever known. Tough but terribly tender, her earthy heart made allowances for human frailty and found a way to help people no matter what.

At first, I thought it was another squall of wind but a low roaring noise kept getting louder. Then I knew. I looked up into the far-reaching Texas sky and saw it. There was a jet stream overhead leaving a white trail against the pale blue. It was like an arrow shooting into my thoughts, reminding me I must leave in a few days and return to Rebekah, Jed, and Luke and my home back in Nashville. My young children were a world away from these wheat fields, the ol' shack, and the half century of hard times that Ruby had faced. Without doubt, my little ones would grow up into a troubled world with hardships of a new kind to overcome, but this Texas pioneer woman stood for courage and hope and I would tell stories about her to them. Ruby had overcome so much. So could I. And, so could my children.

We still had about a mile to walk together. The chilly wind was at our backs making our steps home easier. Ruby looked over at me and laughed, "Can ya stand some more of my cookin'?"

Ruby's Potato Salad and Beans

The main thing I fix for Homer is potato salad and red beans. Whenever I make potato salad, I cream my potatoes. I don't dice 'em. Then I put apple cider vinegar, salt, and pepper, onions, and pickles, and boiled eggs, and I jus' stir it up and that's the kind he likes.

Whenever ya cook yer potatoes, drain the juice off of 'em and put it in a cup and instead of havin' mayonnaise for a dressin', jus put more of that juice back in it.

I've been a cookin' since I was eleven years old and this is the way I always made it. That's the way my mother fixed 'em and that's the way I fix 'em.

Now the red beans. I jus' pick 'em (pick the rocks out of 'em) and wash 'em. Use two cups red beans, four cups water and I usually put salt pork in 'em, and I jus let 'em cook. I don't put any salt in 'em cause of that pork. Homer can't have too much salt. I jus' let 'em cook real slow until they get good and tender. It takes quite a while. Ya don't cook 'em fast, but ya start 'em fast, then just turn 'em down.

Ya know it causes gas more on some people than it does others, but jus put ya a pinch of soda in it when ya start to cook 'em, and that takes care of it.

&a   &a   &a

Chapter Four

Best wishes from Tennessee Martha Belle 1990

MARTHA, THE TENNESSEE BELLE

HELLO, BA-A-W-BRA?" the cheerful voice sang on the other end of the telephone. "What ya doin' ta-night? I got front row tickets ta a country music awards show in Nashville an' how bout droppin' everything, an' let's go?"

"Where? What time? I'll have to get a babysitter for the kids since this is a school night," I clamored, my mind running with all the arrangements I'd have to make in order to go on the spur of the moment. But, I wanted to go and seldom passed up the chance to have a night out on the town. Besides, my neighbor and friend, Martha Belle, who had been a widow since 1976, was more fun than a teenager and nearly as daring even though she was close to her sixty-fifth birthday.

"Get yaw-self dolled-up cause it's at Opryland Hotel in one a' those fan-ca ballrooms an' there'll be lots a' people there. Lots a' big stars," she said. "And ya never know who ya' might see."

We talked about what each of us would wear, getting away early enough to eat dinner together at a Chinese restaurant, and that I would drive my car. Martha did not like to drive at night. Since she lived down the road

91

about a mile or so, on a nearby farm, it would take me less than five minutes to drive to her house, then about forty-five minutes to drive from our tiny town of Spring Hill to the Opryland Hotel in Nashville. *Oh boy! This would be great fun.*

I was raring to go. My hair was freshly washed and full, my facial makeup smooth and blended just right. The tailored, red wool dress I slipped on made me feel smart and stylish. It was almost ankle length, and there was a long colorful scarf draped over my left shoulder to highlight the dress. Martha had not seen this particular dress because it had been hanging in my closet since the last time I visited friends in Dallas, Texas. The low black heels on my feet matched a small leather clutchbag.

Although I felt well dressed, I knew Martha Belle would twinkle like a star in her new navy knit dress with the big white lace collar and clustered pearl earrings. She had a flair and elegance with clothes and color, but it was her dynamic smile and personality that made her stand out in any group. Wherever Martha Belle appeared, she attracted people like a magnet. She stood about 5' 7", carrying her 140 pounds in all the right places, and wore her silver-white hair cut short and curly. Her dark-toned skin had remained smooth and youthful looking against her round dancing eyes. They were hazel. Martha Belle's eyes talked as much as her voice and were always warm and full of emotion unless she got stirred up or angry about something. Then, they shot bullets.

With one phone call, I was able to reach my regular babysitter, Zephyr Fite, who would arrive any minute to spend the evening with my children. I was anxious to fly out the back door of the farm house but had to tell Zephyr about a pipe leaking under the kitchen sink, how six long-horned cattle had jumped the cattleguard and were dumping cowpiles in the backyard, and to keep the kids away from the cows, as well as the piles, and that I was out of milk.

Zephyr, who was now in her seventies, had helped care for my children since 1984, before Luke was born, as well as throughout the last two years of my troubled personal life. She never had children of her own and had been a widow for many years, so my babies were like Zephyr's own grandchildren. Zephyr lived alone on a small farm further out in the country. She raised a big garden, tended a small herd of cattle, sat with sick neighbors, carried food to shut-ins, and was as busy as any career woman. Yet, whenever I called her to babysit, she never failed to drive the twenty minutes to help out.

"Aw-w-w, have a good time," Zephyr said. She was always straight forward. "And don't worry about nothin' cause it won't matter a hundred years from now!" She smiled after me as I hurried down the sidewalk, jumped in my car, and left a trail of gravel flying in the air as I drove away. I zoomed passed the fruit trees, the one-hundred-year-old hackberry tree, across the bumpy cattleguard, and over the springfed creek toward Martha Belle's.

I thought to myself, *Thank the Good Lord a million times for Zephyr*, who was as stable and solid as that ancient hackberry tree. I don't know how I would have made it the past couple of years taking care of three small children, alone, without her. One of these days, I was going to tell Zephyr how much she meant to me.

Meanwhile, there was a night of fun and music ahead. And, I had to pick up Martha Belle.

ﺏ ﺏ ﺏ

A historic marker stood discreetly at the corner of Martha Belle's long winding drive. It was a tall, black metal pole with a small sign on the top, bordered in wrought-iron. The sign read, "Hood's Haven, built 1832." Also at the entrance was a hand-stacked stone fence made before the Civil War. It reached about four feet high. The historic marker and stone fence were glimpses of things to come, further down the road.

Driving down Martha Belle's narrow lane was like entering the movie set for "Gone with the Wind," or turning back the pages of time to the old, old South. Back to the yesterdays of great plantations, endless fields of cotton, grand parties, taffeta dresses which covered layers of petticoats and hoops, banana curls, wealthy ladies with creamy white skin, and gentlemen farmers riding sleek horses surveying their cash crops and negro slaves.

Martha Belle's home had as much colorful history in real life as Scarlett O'Hara's plantation did in the movie. It was here, on this plantation, that Lt. General John B. Hood, commander of the Confederate Army in Tennessee, and his staff spent the night using Martha Belle's house as a command post because it sat on the highest hill in the area. They could see all around. General Hood was ordered to capture Nashville and cut off the Union Army from supplies. General Hood was only thirty miles south of Nashville and taking control of the route to Nashville was strategic.

However, during that fateful night of November 29, 1864, General Hood had suffered a brief illness. While he slept in a giant Victorian bed in the downstairs bedroom in Martha Belle's house, his soldiers were camped nearby. The story is told that his men were tired and drinking that night. Then, the Union Army, under the command of General John Schofield, slipped by the Confederates' campfires and made their way north to Franklin.

The next day, on November 30, 1864, one of the bloodiest battles of the war was fought, just fifteen miles north of Martha Belle's. More officers were killed or wounded in this siege than in any other battle of the Civil War. The Confederates lost six generals, and eighty-five hundred men fell in less than an hour. The end of the Civil War came just five months after General Hood's night in Martha Belle's house.

But she liked living here and was not disturbed by the historic secrets hidden in the three-brick-thick walls. Every brick in her antebellum home had been handmade from clay, dug from the edge of the four-acre lake behind one of the barns. Many of Martha Belle's friends and relatives wished she would move because the house was so big and needed constant maintenance. The rooms were large and square with fourteen-foot ceilings downstairs and eighteen-foot ceilings upstairs, and the entry hallway had a ceiling forty feet tall. The wide planked floors were ash and poplar.

Although she had each room furnished in period Victorian pieces, true to its time, the romantic aura of the house was clouded with plumbing problems, inch-wide cracks in the walls, plaster needing to be replaced, and outdoor deterioration from weather and age. Over a hundred years of violent storms, floods, and tornadoes had swept across middle Tennessee and over her 340 acres, beating against the stately house. Each storm had left its mark from one end of Martha Belle's farm to the other. Several century old oaks, massive and towering, had been pulled up by their roots, and they lay like fallen kings across the front pastures. Fat Hereford cattle grazed quietly around them.

Down the half mile lane I drove, dodging deep potholes when a baby rabbit jumped out of a tobacco field on the right and hopped onto the road. This was the same dirt road traveled by Confederate soldiers on horseback, slaves in buckboard wagons, and Southern gentlemen in two-seater buggies. But today, on this road my foot mashed the brakes in my comfortable car to keep from hitting a rabbit.

When I reached the end, there was Martha Belle's grand place. Flowering dogwood, redbud, walnut, hackberry, poplar, ash, and oak trees grew all around the yard. Like proud guardians, the most impressive trees were the 150-year-old waxy magnolia trees. The State Forestry Department had told her those magnolia trees were the largest and oldest anywhere in the South. Underneath their shade, patches of yellow buttercups, azaleas, and hyacinths blanketed the ground. Big boxwoods grew along the brick walkway to the front porch where four white square columns reached all the way to the top of the two story house and stood sturdy and valiant against antiquated red bricks and grey shutters. This was truly a magnificient house on a high hill. It looked stately in the yellow sun at day's end. Although Hood's Haven belonged to the past, it welcomed me with pride and dignity everytime I drove up the lane to come for a visit. And, I had made many visits and spent many hours with Martha Belle and her three married daughters, their families, and other friends in this place.

"I love livin' here," Martha Belle mused. "I can see everythin' around me. If I lived in town, I wouldn't know who was comin'." She looked across the horizon lined with tobacco and wheat fields, squinted her eyes with pleasure and continued. "I sleep with ma upstairs winda open at night cause it faces tha east an' I can see tha risin' sun in tha mornin' an' see tha moon go across at night." Her voice trailed off in slow motion. "I like tha night sounds, tha honkin' a geese, doves, owls, an' frogs. People always ask me if I'm afraid here in this big house." She shook her head back and forth.

"Ma stars an' garters! . . . No-o-o!" She acted like it was ridiculous for anyone to worry about living in a giant antebellum. "Why, tha sheriff patrols this road aw-w-l-l tha time," she drawled. "An' tha po-lice even cawl me on tha phone ta check on me. I surela appreciate them doin' that," she said. As if it were a closed case, she concluded, "And God an' His angels aw looking ova me."

We needed to hurry. I honked the horn for Martha Belle as I pulled my car to a stop in front of a mounted dinner bell beside the back door. This bell was used years ago to call workmen or field hands home for dinner. It could be heard for miles. Martha used the bell to call her grandchildren from fishing in the lake, or hiking across the fields to see giant flocks of Canadian geese. At one time, there were over four hundred geese on her lake.

Martha Belle peeped through the kitchen window and waved. There was a broad grin on her face, as usual. I could see she was talking on the telephone. Shortly, she stuck her head out the back door and hollered for me to wait just a minute.

"Let me find ma earscrews," she shouted from the steps. She dashed away while I sat with the car running. Martha Belle was forever misplacing her reading glasses and rushing around to find them at the last minute, so I was not surprised to see she had misplaced her earrings. It didn't matter. She was a busy and successful real estate agent, and I understood she had a lot of things on her mind. Often, I teased her and told her she needed a telephone implanted in her ear.

Waiting and looking out the window of my car, I checked my wristwatch for the time and then noticed the

apple tree not far from where I was parked. The tree really
was Martha Belle's. One day back in 1977 she had been
mowing the yard on her tractor and had just eaten an apple.

"Gee. This is sa good, I'm just gonna bury this core, an
up came that tree," she chuckled. The large branches were
now heavy with white blossoms, and bees buzzed all
around.

Martha Belle finally appeared. She hurried and locked
the back door and rushed to the car. "Whew-w-w! Let's go
bafore that phone rings again!" Martha Belle laughed and
sighed at the same time as she bounced into the front
seat. Her good smelling perfume filled the car. "Ma
mother awl-ways told me I was born with ma hat on." Her
hazel eyes popped with excitement. "An', I like ta prove
her right."

Martha Belle looked beautiful in her new navy knit
dress as she reached to buckle the seat belt. Her hands
were nervous as she fumbled to lock the belt in place. Her
silver hair looked airy and glistened in the afternoon light.
Martha Belle took another deep breath, looked me in the
eye, then with her usual quick grin, she said, "Let's scoot!"

And, away we went to Nashville.

ða ða ða

It was the fall of 1981. There was a black and white
photograph in the newspaper of a young man and woman
sitting at a table signing books. The caption under the
picture read, "Authors of *The Walk West* autograph books
as part of a national publicity tour." The authors were on
a forty-five city tour with four autograph parties in Nashville, Tennessee. This tour pushed *The Walk West* to number four on the New York Times bestseller list, and Martha Belle Smith was one of the book buyers standing in

the long line at the Green Hills bookstore where 150 books had already been sold. She had been standing almost an hour.

Halfway into the autographing, she approached the table stacked with crisp new books right off the press. She wore a smile that only a true Southerner could give. It was broad, welcoming, and as warm as a June day.

"He-e-l-l-o," she cooed. "Ma name is Maw-w-tha Belle Smith, an' I'm sa da-lighted ta meet ya." She politely extended her hand. Her voice had a drawl as long as the line of people waiting to buy books. "I'm known as tha land lady a' real estate an I'd like ta see ya come ta Tenn-a-sea. I'll help ya find a fawm here." She handed me her business card, Southern-style, then asked to have her books autographed.

This was the first time I set eyes on Martha Belle, and she impressed me, but I never dreamed I'd ever see her again. I figured she was one of those energetic real estate agents, eager to sell something. Or, she was a reader of adventure books and had read the walk across America stories in *National Geographic Magazine* or *Readers Digest*. Whatever her motives, I tucked her business card in my purse and forgot about it. At that time, living in Tennessee was the farthest thing from my mind because New Orleans was my home.

Then to my surprise, almost a year passed and one hot July day in 1982, Martha Belle Smith had nine pieces of farm property in middle Tennessee lined up to show. With a three year old daughter, Rebekah, and a new baby on the way, it was time to decide where to raise a family. And, although I loved the sultry city of New Orleans, I wanted my children to have a rural/country lifestyle but live close enough to a major city to have the cultural advantages.

With Martha Belle leading the way to Tennessee, a part of me wanted to stay behind in the cresent city of New Orleans because of my youthful days of courtship and marriage. They had been free and magical. I would never forget the sultry breezes, the chicory coffee, succulent seafood, jazz, The French Quarter, roaming artists and dancers, exotic plants and hotels, fishing boats, street cars, mansions under regal live oaks, and the many friends I had known. I'd never forget working on a master's degree at the New Orleans Baptist Theological Seminary and all my smart professors. They all mingled together in my memory, sort of murky and marvelous, but always enchanting and forever young.

Just as the mighty Mississippi River was always moving on, it was time for me to do the same. There was more to think about than the constant beat of soul music and fanciful dreams. New Orleans, the city that never sleeps, was like a giant spider, weaving its watery webb of nightlife and passion to catch its prey, but Martha Belle and the gentle countryside of Tennessee was calling me to a new life.

"Ten-n-na-sea is a place where ya can drop a seed anywhere an it'll come up," Martha Belle cheered. I questioned if she was secretly with the Chamber of Commerce. To be such a sophisticated and professional woman, she sure enjoyed showing farms and open land. Even though she had long, painted fingernails, classy earrings, and wore open-toed heels, she moved across grassy fields and pastures with ease. Where did she learn to do that?

When asked if the farm land in this region was fertile, Martha blurted, "Ab-b-so-o-lut—la!" She drew that word out into at least six syllables. "Ma stars . . . any seed will grow if ya just put it in tha ground!"

At that time, Martha Belle drove a big blue Cadillac, as big and long as a submarine. She needed a crash helmet, along with the seat belt, because she drove that tank Cadillac as fast as a race car. We flew down Interstate 65, (I was afraid to look at the speedometer), making a quick right turn onto a narrow two-lane road. She wanted to show a farm less than forty-five minutes from the airport and only thirty miles south of Nashville.

"Where is this farm?" I asked.

"Yaw not gonna ba-lieve it, but it's down tha road from ma fawm and just come on tha mawket yestaday." Her voice was bubbly but always Southern. "And, I ba-lieve it's what ya want. Even has an old white fawm house on it."

We passed one white farm house after another, old home places where early settlers had once lived. They had front porches with swings and rocking chairs and rows and rows of blooming pink impatiens, red petunias, purple violets, and other flowers. Most often a clothesline was strung out back, many full of sheets dragging the ground and getting whiter in the July sun. Some places still had big black iron kettles in the yard where women in the old days boiled their laundry.

Martha Belle, dressed in a bright blue suit, giggled like a carefree child, pointing out blackberry bushes, honeysuckle vines, and flowers. This woman was as colorful in her personality as all those flowers. What was it about her? I knew she was a widow, a real estate agent, and she mentioned she had three grown daughters and some grandchildren. But she seemed so happy all the time. Why? When the moment was right, I planned to find out more. She was probably one of those aristocratic Southern women with lots of money and never had any serious problems like most of us have.

We topped a high ridge. Martha Belle slammed on her Cadillac brakes, jerking us forward. Dust flew everywhere.

"Oops!" she laughed. She covered her mouth to muffle the giggles. "Don't let me scare ya." I swallowed hard, thankful we hadn't gone over the cliff.

There in front of us spread a wide valley, like a handsome antique quilt made up of different sized fields—patches of green clover and alfalfa, brown blocks of wheat and corn, muddy barn lots with slow moving horses and mules, and rolling Tennessee hills covered in woods. Here and there were round blue-green ponds fed by underground springs and farm houses that had withstood hard winters and hot summers.

As if we had seen enough, Martha Belle stomped her foot on the gas and we were off, tearing up the country road in her Cadillac, and before I could catch my breath, she turned into a nondescript driveway, bounced us across a worn metal cattleguard, and then stopped with another jolt in the middle of a narrow concrete bridge. When I looked out, there were no side rails on the bridge. Below us, straight down, was a winding, rushing creek full of swift water and big rocks. If I opened the car door, there wasn't room to stand without falling off the bridge.

"There's lots of water on this fawm, includin' this creek that's flooded ova this bridge bafore," she warned. My eyes got wider. This was one daring woman. Just as I looked out the window and down at a school of minnows in the clear swift water, Martha Belle peeled out again.

She stopped at the end of a long gravel driveway in front of a white, two-story farm house, at least one hundred years old. The house looked like it belonged in a Norman Rockwell painting. A cloud of summer dust settled around the Cadillac. When I could see clearly, I noticed the yard was full of princely maple trees. They shaded the simple farmhouse from the burning sun.

After we walked around the property and toured the old house, I told Martha Belle I liked this farm very much. It seemed a good place to raise my children—how it was close enough to the airport and the city, but still in the country. She then dropped her Southern smile and pulled off her sunglasses. I could see her hazel eyes were locked in place. She looked me straight in the eye with a sober stare. In her drawl, which was even longer in the July heat, she said, "If ya want it . . . ya . . . betta . . . get . . . it . . . *taday!*"

Her eyes weren't dancing, and she wasn't giggling. Her face was fixed and serious. "It's priced ta sell." Something told me when it came to making a deal and doing business, Martha Belle didn't pull any punches or mince with short, or long, words. She might be a widow, she might be a woman, she might be over fifty-five, she might be Southern, but she was aw-w-l business.

Sure enough, the next day there were four other buyers lined up at the real estate office to buy the same farm, but speedy Martha Belle had taken a contract and earnest money to the owners first. She knew the farm was priced to sell. Not a moment too late, that farm became my home in July, 1982 and Martha Belle Smith, who lived down the road about a mile and a half in the historic Hood's Haven, became my neighbor.

೩ ೩ ೩

I was driving, not as fast as Martha Belle, but I was driving. We sped north on I-65 and made the loop around Nashville headed toward Briley Parkway to the Opryland Hotel. We had eighteen minutes until the country music awards show. Nashville was quietly important to Martha Belle because she and her late husband, Dr. John R.

Smith, lived here for ten years. They lived on Glen Leven Drive, down the street from famous stars like Minnie Pearl, Webb Pierce, Dorothy and Tex Ritter, and even the Governor's Mansion. Martha knew this town from every angle. She had been in garden clubs, fashion shows, church programs, active in politics, and was busy in school events back during the years while raising her three daughters.

Martha Belle knew Nashville was well-rounded with its private academic schools, art galleries, and Vanderbilt Hospital and University where Southern literature was taught with determination (from the fine writing of Robert Penn Warren to Alex Haley). Nashville had the only replica of the Athens Parthenon, built in 1897 for the Tennessee Centennial, and there was Fort Nashboro on the bluffs of the Cumberland River (a reproduction from 1780 when the Cherokees attacked it), the Tennessee Performing Arts Center where popular Broadway productions from New York played, Botanical Gardens at Cheekwood, Southern mansions like Belle Meade, and much, much more. For all of Nashville's culture, Martha Belle was perfectly clear about one thing.

"People don't come here from aw-w-l-l ova tha world ta see plays, aw read books, aw see schools," Martha quipped. "They come ta see tha Gran-n-n-d . . . Ol' . . . Opr-r-ra an' hear countra music!" she said as we walked with a clip up the steps of the elaborate Opryland Hotel. I couldn't wait to get inside, find the ballroom, and see all the big name stars.

I leaned over and whispered in Martha's ear. "A lot of people think country music is corny."

"Ma . . . Hea-a-a-vens!" Martha shouted, slowly. People in the lobby turned and looked at us. "I grew up with countra music an if ya listen ta it, it tells a story. Like Dolly Parton's song about a coat of mana colors."

Like most adults, I knew country music was not lofty or sophisticated compared to classical music. Martha Belle explained how country music originally came from ballads in England and Scotland, but here in the USA, it came out of the hearts and hills and lives of Southerners look-ing for a way to express their lonesome and heartsick themes. From Virginia to Texas, the simple sounds of gui-tars and fiddles and pleading voices captured the soul of America and eventually the world. From its start in the early days of radio in the 1920s, country music was now listened to by over 150 million people.

"I rememba back when ma daddy saved up an' bought a little small radio. We could onla play it on Saturda nights ta listen ta The Grand Ol' Opry, an' we'd all go ta sleep a listenin' ta it."

Fans had spent more than 550 million dollars on re-corded music last year alone. Country music wasn't corny—it was big, big business. With over half the popu-lation in the United States as listeners, the airwaves stayed loaded with songs about broken lives, Mama's hun-gry eyes, whiskey drinkin' men, bein' poor, holdin' your baby close, tight fittin' jeans, lookin' for love over a bar stool, D-I-V-O-R-C-E, fallin' to pieces, takin' off your weddin' band for the night, workin' hard all week, lovin' her but wishin' it was you, growin' old but stayin' young, satin sheets, dying, crying, heartaches and heartbreak and more heartaches. This music was the guts of life. Love found and love lost. Suffering. And dreams.

No one will ever know the number of small town or country young men and women who have lain awake at night—looking up at the stars from a sleeping house, lis-tening to crickets and pond frogs, but pushed by their talent and stirred by their trouble, and dreaming of city lights—have envisioned themselves being on stage at the Grand Ol' Opry. The cries of these dreamers, those who beat the odds and made it, have touched the core of life. Their lyrics hit common ground. Any person who has lived long enough to be bruised by love, hate, death, sorrow, and hard times can identify with the stories told in country music.

Especially my southern friend, Martha Belle.

ᏸ ᏸ ᏸ

To know Martha Belle now, living in a big antebellum home, driving a luxury car, and greeting real estate clients with a successful smile, no one would guess the struggles she had faced or the meager beginnings from which she came. This gracious woman was born in a little wooden shanty on the edge of the Tennessee Smokey Mountains. It was a freezing February day back in 1925 when the country doctor arrived. The shack was drafty and the ground outside was covered in deep snow. An ice-covered creek flowed silently nearby. The women relatives gathered together to help, keeping the coal fires stoked and water boiling on the stove. One of the women, Aunt Laura, was also a registered nurse. She had traveled through the cold mountains to assist the doctor with the delivery.

When Martha Belle was finally born on that blustery winter day, Aunt Laura wrapped the baby in a thick hand-made blanket and held her close to keep the infant from freezing to death. Martha Belle's parents, Lee and Ethel Lambert, had already suffered a terrible loss over the death of their firstborn child, a baby girl who died of pneumonia at eighteen months of age. So their second born, Martha

Belle Lambert, was a blessing to the grief-stricken family, and her tiny new life had to be saved no matter what. Unknowingly, Martha Belle helped mend wounded hearts and from that day on, whenever winter storms would blow in from the north, someone in the Lambert family would remember, "It's almost as cold as the day when Martha Belle was born."

Those early years were spent in the mountains, a place tucked away from the world where little girls could run free and the only dangers were from wild animals and not people. The place was called "Happy Valley." Martha Belle, a quiet child, played as much as she could in clear creeks and deep swimming holes, sliding down high hills in old rubber tires, catching fireflies at dark, reading by kerosene lamps because there was no electricity in the house, and walking three miles to the grist mill with her grandfather to have big ears of corn ground into cornmeal. And on Sundays, she walked the dirt road to a little church on a hilltop always wearing the same dress.

"Motha made me a Sunda dress. It was floral and loose and she made it with a big hem sa she could keep lettin' it down. I wore that dress until I was ten or twelve," Martha Belle said. "I wore it evra Sunda. They didn't have ta see ma face cause they'd know it was me from ma dress." Since four children were born after her, Martha Belle became a second mother. She was kept busy baking biscuits, cooking corn and beans, carrying water from a rock spring, and helping take care of the house and other kids. There was always work to do and people to feed. And very little money.

Martha Belle laughed, "I grew up with a Sears Roebuck catalog an' a little house out back." She cut her eyes over at me and they twinkled. "If ya know what I'm a talkin' about, and boy!" she took a deep breath, "was it cold when ya went out there in tha wint-a."

Martha Belle's father was a rugged outdoorsman and worked hard in sawmills to support his growing family. When more children came along, he began crushing stone and helping build roads across the hills of West Virginia, North Carolina, and Georgia. He had to go wherever there was work. The family and what few goods they owned were packed up, and Martha Belle spent the first five years of her elementary grades in different schools. She never regretted moving from town to town and school to school.

She remarked, "I've had many real estate clients tell ma they didn't want ta move cause they wanted ta keep their children in tha same school." She paused to shake her head back and forth. I knew she had more to say. Although Martha Belle was a gentle lady, she was strong when it came to some things. "Ya never know when ya go in-ta a place who yaw gonna meet, who will help ya-aw child, and ma theory is ta never fear movin' or changin'."

She cleared her throat and darted her eyes. Her mind turned constantly with thoughts and ideas and opinions. "Progress means change—in yaw work, in yaw school, developin' personalities, meetin' people—and ya have got ta learn how ta do that."

One day Martha Belle's father looked down at his daughter who had never spent an entire year in the same school and said it was time for his family to stop moving around. She was in the fifth grade when they settled in Maryville, Tennessee. For the first time in her childhood, life became settled with the same friends, school, and home. Martha Belle finished high school there. Living close to Knoxville, she entered the University of Tennessee and later graduated from Tennessee Tech in Cookeville with a degree in Home Economics and Science. The year was 1948.

After college, she rode a ferry to cross rushing mountain rivers and find backwoods homes of isolated women who needed her help. Martha Belle became a Home Demonstration Agent. She met with people in schools, on farms, at 4-H clubs, and wherever there was a need to learn more about cooking, canning, freezing, sewing, and making life easier for homemakers. She knew, firsthand, how tough it was to survive with very little, so she taught women homemaking skills from food preservation to weaving cane bottomed chairs.

But then it happened. She fell in love.

"Love is tha most mysterious thing in tha world," she sang. Her voice raised in pitch and was full of feeling. "It was a pourin' rain that day. I met him at ma best friend's weddin' an' it was love at first sight. We both knew it, an' I married him four months lata."

Martha Belle was swept off her mountain feet by the handsome young doctor, John R. Smith from Lafayette, Tennessee. They married in October, 1949, and life for the young Martha Belle changed dramatically. She was picked like a wild flower from the mountains and thrown into the world of medicine, hospitals, doctors, and patients.

Dr. Smith was in general practice in a small east Tennessee town where he did everything from deliver babies to fix broken bones. Every farmer, teacher, logger, and townsperson from miles around called on "Dr. Johnny" when they needed help. When Martha Belle was a poor little girl, dragging a long cotton sack behind her as she picked cotton in the hot Georgia fields, she had thought about becoming a nurse, but she never dreamed she'd marry a doctor who had so many patients that she would have to turn into a "nurse" on some occasions.

One afternoon, Dr. Johnny was gone on a house call. Back in those days, doctors took their little black bags and called on sick folks at home throughout the countryside. There was a knock at Martha Belle's door. An excited man stuttered to say his wife was ready to have a baby, and they needed Dr. Johnny, *quick!* Martha Belle hurried to the old crank phone and turned the handle as fast as she could. She called Pauline, the operator.

"Paw-line!" Martha Belle shouted. "Do ya know wha Dr. Johnna is?"

Everyone in the small town knew the good doctor. Of course, the operator never listened in on anyone's conversations, but somehow, she knew what was going on.

"I just heard Mrs. Watson say he passed her house a few minutes ago. He's on tha county road an' I'll catch him at tha next house," Pauline answered in a hurry.

Martha Belle told the desperate man at her front door to take his wife to the clinic, and she would meet them there because the regular nurse was out of town for the weekend. Martha Belle raced to the clinic to prepare the woman for delivery.

"I took tha lady on tha table, and she was ready ta deliver. This was her twelfth baby," Martha Belle laughed. "It was gonna come any minute, and I kept tellin' her to hold back. Finally, I realized it was a comin' an' I told her to push. Pu-u-ush!"

The mountain woman on the table looked up and over her swollen stomach at Martha Belle. The pregnant woman's face was dripping in sweat, and she was panting. "Are you a nurse, Miss Martha?"

"Heavens no-o-o, I'm a Home Demonstration Agent . . . PU-U-U-SH!" Martha Belle hollered.

About that time, the door opened, and Dr. Johnny walked in. There Martha Belle stood, the temporary nurse, holding a newborn baby. She had never been so glad to see her doctor husband and handed the baby over to him.

(right) "After we married in '33, we lived in this ol' shack over a year," said Ruby.

Ruby fixes Homer's favorite potato salad.

(overleaf) In spite of tornadoes, heat, and drought, Ruby still loves her West Texas ranch.

Ruby and Homer play dominoes with old friends.

"I come to Texas in a covered wagon back in 1915."

Built in 1832, Martha Belle's home was a Civil War command post.

(left) Martha, the Tennessee Belle.

As a widow, it took ten years and hard work, but Martha became one of the top real estate salespeople in the Mid-South.

As a young preacher in 1949, Curtis Eaker took Laverne from the backwoods to be his wife.

(left) Laverne, the preacher's wife.

"C'mon, let's show 'em how to sing," Laverne said.

An oil refinery supervisor, Bob enjoys his flower garden on the weekends. "He grows 'em and I pick 'em," laughs Jan.

(right) Live oaks grow along the bayou and surround Jan's backyard.

"Our problem as women is that we've been taught there's supposed to be zip-zap and fireworks in relationships," Jan said as she and Sharon dry dishes.

Rebekah and MeMe talk about Christmas dinner over the hot wood cookstove.

Rebekah holds
Boots, the gray cat.

(right) Betty, better
known as "MeMe."

Lucy Adele and her husband, Jack, stand near one of Southern Idaho's many potato cellars.

(right) Lucy Adele, Idaho's fair lady.

"She likes me 'cause she gives me hugs and reads to me," said Tavee, the third grade boy.

Like a castle wall, the snow-capped Rocky Mountains watch over Buckshot and the Vickers

Lake City still has the feel gold mining, pistol packin' town.

Buckshot sits on an old twirl-top stool while her hands float across the keyboard.

Emma Jean, "Buckshot." *(overleaf)*

The next twenty-seven years were packed with hundreds of patients, a growing practice, building a new hospital in Lafayette, Tennessee, moving to Atlanta, Georgia, to further John's medical training in ophthalmology, moving to Nashville, and raising a family. The years were crammed with travel, and work, and people, and being on call twenty-four hours a day to the point of exhaustion. When there didn't seem to be a way to stretch the days into more hours, and just when all human energy was gone, another tragedy hit Martha Belle's parents. Her younger sister was killed in a car wreck and left a six-month-old baby girl, Clara.

Martha Belle's parents were getting older, so she took the crippled baby to love and raise as her own. Clara was adopted and became a sister to Martha Belle's other daughters, Jennie and Laura. Day after day, year after year, Martha Belle worked and struggled with the growing Clara to teach her to walk on a twisted leg and foot, how to use a damaged arm and hand, and tutored her in school. With three daughters to raise, a busy doctor to help, school, church, and politics, Martha Belle stayed busier than the bees that swarmed her flower garden. Time passed too fast.

And times changed. Things started changing when Dr. Johnny fell sick. Like other compassionate doctors, the long hours and care for hundreds of patients were stronger than his care for himself. He had pushed himself too hard to meet the needs of his patients—losing sleep, eating poorly, and enduring pressure. To slow down, Martha Belle and her overworked husband made plans to get away from Nashville but before they could, Dr. Johnny was hit with spinal meningitis.

His tired body became inflamed and ballooned to twice his normal size. Baptist Hospital in Nashville had to build a tent to keep the sheets off his bursting skin. His condition was so severe and so unusual, student doctors arrived to study the disease. Months later, in a weakened condition, Dr. Johnny recovered long enough to go back to work and move to the country. But he was never a strong man again.

Martha Belle sold their Nashville home that was down the street from Minnie Pearl to another famous country-music singer and movie star, Jerry Reed, and then, ironically, bought the historic antebellum, Hood's Haven, from one more set of country music stars, George Jones and Tammy Wynette. She and Dr. Johnny were finally in the country—safe at last. Except for the huge medical bills from her husband's illness and his mounting business debts, they could really live and enjoy life and be together. Now they lived where there was nothing except green farm land in every direction.

"This is the best deal we ever made and if we have to let everything else go, we can feed our children and grandchildren," Dr. Johnny said. "We've sent our children abroad. Now you and I are going to Europe, Hawaii, and different places." He smiled at his happy wife that morning over coffee, looking across the warm October fields that had been harvested and listening to birds singing their wake-up songs. He planned to meet Martha Belle on the lake to fish when he came home from work that afternoon. Then he left their quiet plantation for the hospital and his office in Nashville.

"I had a urgent feelin' ta call John," Martha Belle said softly. "I knew he had ta do two surgeries that mornin', but I got this feelin' I had ta talk ta him." She took several deep breaths. She looked away, then lowered her silver-haired head. "I got a hold of his receptionist an' she kept a tellin' me ta hold on. I said I had ta talk ta my husband." Martha Belle raised her hazel eyes toward me, and they were flooded with old pain and fresh tears. She spoke in hushed tones that seemed to echo off the Civil War walls.

"Finally, tha receptionist came on tha line an' she was a cryin'." Martha Belle stopped and tried to swallow the lump in her throat. We sat silent at her kitchen table across from each other in the enormous antebellum house. Only the pendulum from a grandfather clock moved. Tears rolled down her cheeks and dropped on the table. In a whisper and a cracked voice, she finished, "The receptionist said, 'Honey, Dr. Johnny can't come ta tha phone . . . He just died.' "

Martha Belle stared at me with a face full of memories and a heart too tender to touch. "He collapsed an' died right then," she snapped her fingers and turned her head away. He died of a massive heart attack on October 15, 1976. I only listened while she wept.

ə ə ə

The two of us stood in the swarming, glitsy crowd. Martha Belle and I were all dolled up in our expensive, tailored clothes outside the giant ballroom at the Opryland Hotel. Martha Belle was smiling from ear to ear and punching me to notice certain people walk by. This was not our usual Sunday school crowd. I had never seen so many glittery clothes and sequins. My expensive wool dress that came down to my ankles, which I thought was beautiful, looked plain next to the dresses other women wore.

One woman, thirty something, sashayed in front of me wearing a skin-tight red leather skirt and jacket with a plunging blouse to reveal her big bouncing bosom. The shiny leather skirt was shorter than a pair of summer shorts with a slit up the back, and the woman's long legs

reminded me of a black spider. She wore silver earrings
that hung down to her shoulders like shimmering icicles
on a Christmas tree. They were at least three inches long.
Her hair was bleached yellow-white and cut very short
like a man's, in a spiked haircut. In Colorado, I had seen
porcupines with shorter spikes.

Martha Belle shot her dancing eyes over at me and we
both had to look the other way to keep from laughing.
We must have looked strange to her too. That is, if she
saw us.

Young and old were there, men and women dressed
from casual to gaudy to formal. Some of the faces were
mainstream America, others looked rich or elite, and some
looked hard and tired. The troubles of life could be seen
in the deep furrows and creases on the faces of some people, especially the older women. Their thick makeup and
colored eyelids didn't cover their rough lives, and I understood why country music soothed their souls. It would
help them release their pent-up feelings, make them
happy or make them cry. I was sure many of them had
struggled and worked hard to make it in this world, and I
wondered how many of them were divorced like me, or
were widows, like Martha Belle.

"Vera few people go through life without problems,"
Martha Belle said. "Evera mountain ya cross will make ya
stronger for tha next one so ya can face the future. Ya
gotta realize yaw gonna have problems. If I hadn't had all
these debts and holes ta fill up, I'd have been awl-right,
but ya don't have ta face em alone," she declared. "Keep
yaw faith in God an' keep workin' toward tha future cause
ya don't know what's out there a waitin' for ya."

Martha Belle had a lot of mountains to cross, being
left alone at the age of fifty, with a handicapped daughter
in high school, Laura off in college, medical bills not cov-

ered by insurance, business debts to cover, the farm mort-
gage, and a broken heart. She knew there had to be a way
to make it. Martha Belle had survived a hard life years ago
back in the Smoky Mountains. Now, she could do it again.

The year following Dr. Johnny's death, she attended
college at night to train in real estate. She drove herself to
succeed, working seven days a week pushing property,
meeting people, listing houses and farms, and selling. She
did so well, she became the top salesperson in the company where she worked. In 1986, Martha Belle Smith sold
over 5 million dollars worth of property in Williamson
County and, since then, has become widely known.

"I feel like I've done real well for a matron ta come in,
a woman who hadn't worked 'n this business bafore, 'n tha
world of men, an' I feel pleased I could do sa well."

"You think you have a future, even at your age?" I
asked hesitantly. I didn't want to offend her.

"Oh ma stars, Baw-w-bra! Ya can start a new life at
fifty, sixty, or eighty-five. Yaw life is jus' beginnin'. Why,
ya can start a new life at ninety!" she exclaimed. Martha
Belle threw her head back and laughed. "Jus' give me a
chance!"

Martha Belle nudged me again as a well-dressed man
in a three-piece suit walked by. He looked like he belonged on Wall Street in New York. I thought she wanted
me to notice his good looks but she raised her eyebrows
and looked down. Then I saw the pair of Reebok sneakers
he was wearing. All around the lobby were cowboy hats,
lots of alligator boots, decorated jackets, dyed hair, rhine-
stones, tights, bulky jewelry, and lace. Ladies limped on
heels too high while men with poofed-out hair, sprayed
too stiff to comb, watched from the corner of their eyes.
Hundreds waited for the ballroom doors to open. Cigarette
smoke rose like a signal to hurry up. Everyone was anxious

for the country music awards show to begin, and the air was filled with electricity.

Inside the ballroom, stars like George Jones, Gary Mc-Spadden, Alabama, T. Graham Brown, and Patty Loveless were waiting to perform on stage. Lights and television cameras and loud bands were getting ready. This would be a night of action. I held onto Martha Belle's arm because I didn't want her to get trampled when the massive doors opened. Her heart was racing, and she was ready to get ahead of the crowd to find our reserved seats.

"I don't want to lose you—just yet," I teased.

"When it's ma time ta go, this is as good a-way as any," she grinned back at me, pressing through the people. "When I die, I hope I fall off a horse, I'm in the air, or on tha go," Martha Belle chuckled under her breath. "Take one step on earth an' tha next in Glory!"

With a swoosh, Martha Belle and I were pushed by the crowd through the ballroom doors and there was the green-eyed Patty Loveless on stage with her five-piece band getting ready to sing the number one country music single, "Timber, I'm Falling In Love."

Martha Belle's Polk Salad

Neva, ever, neva, eat polk leaves or stalks raw cause they are poison. Dependin' on tha area, they're found mostla on new ground in the spring time. Go out in tha yard or fields an' pick tha young leaves. Get 'em before it blooms.

Wash 'em thoroughly, rinse ya might say, and use tha tenderest part of tha stalk.

Cover 'em with water, dependin' on how much ya have in tha pot, and bring ta a boil—about two minutes. Drain. Cover again with water an' boil. Drain. Add water tha third time, a vera small amount.

Beat ya two eggs. Put bacon grease in a skillet, add tha cooked, drained polk leaves an' add tha eggs. Cook. Add salt upon servin' with some vinegar an' it's delicious.

I serve it as a main vegetable with a dinna. Lots a times, I go out an' pick it an' cook it an' eat a bowl full myself.

ᔕ ᔕ ᔕ

Chapter Five

THE PREACHER'S COUNTRY WIFE

"Get outta here, you dummy!" the pretty little girl with round grey eyes yelled at her older brother Paul. Laverne was ten years old and the only girl out of five brothers. Holding her own was not easy against a bunch of ornery boys.

"Yer gonna get in trouble, and I'm gonna tell on you!" Laverne snapped at him. He snickered back at her. It was too early in the morning to start a fight, but Laverne was ready for a match with either of her two older brothers, morning, noon, or night.

"B-a-b-y . . ." Paul teased. "Yer just a big b—a—b—y." He spelled out the letters in a sing-song way. Laverne stuck her tongue out at him and kicked dirt on his legs.

"Yer nothin' but a smart alec!" Laverne countered.

Paul was making fun of Laverne because she had to crawl under their three-room farmhouse to collect eggs from the hens who refused to lay eggs in the regular nests. She didn't like this job one bit, but she had to do it. Their farmhouse sat too close to the ground for her two older brothers, Paul or Orville, to get under there and her other three brothers, Irving, Eudell, and Billy, were too young or still in diapers. It was dark and dirty and a tight squeeze. When it came time to gather eggs, Laverne tried to sneak under and get out before the older boys saw her, or they would threaten to pin her under the house. The rising spring sun was just over the horizon, and it wasn't hot yet. It was May, 1944. There were only two more days left of school, then Laverne could do what she really wanted to do. Her dream was to climb the biggest tree on the farm, perch herself in the fork of a limb, and pretend she was a bird. She could sit there until the wind blew and sway back and forth in the breeze. The leaves would rustle, and she could watch them shimmer in the sun. Then she would pretend she had wings and with ease, lift herself up and fly away. She would soar through the peaceful sky, light and airy, and look down on the troubles she had left behind.

Hundreds of chickens scratched in the yard around the small wooden farmhouse, looking for tiny bits of gravel and undiscovered pellets of corn and table scraps. Laverne loved to feed and water the chickens. Most of the grass in the yard grew in patches, and the rest was bare dirt from all the chickens. *Cluck, cluck, cluck* went the noisy chickens. High chirps from baby chicks and strong clucks from old hens were like a steady chorus of a never ending song.

Laverne ignored her brother Paul and bravely set out to gather the eggs. She had already collected over a dozen from the hen house, but now she had to crawl under the farmhouse. She ducked down and wiggled through the small opening. Oh, she hated this but she'd never let Paul know how bad. On her belly, she held her breath and looked all around until her eyes got used to the dark. At least it was cool under the house. The smell of damp earth filled her nose as she prayed she wouldn't see a spider or a rattlesnake. She also had to be careful of broken glass and sharp rocks.

Good. There were three eggs under a floor joist, and within arm's reach were another two eggs nestled in a corner. With five fresh eggs in her hands, she scooted backwards on her belly and made her way out from the dark hole. She squinted her eyes in the spring sunlight and stood up.

Just as she stood up straight, an old bantam rooster let out a fierce crow, flew out of nowhere, and jumped on Laverne. She didn't know what was happening.

"Oh-o-o-o, help, *help!*" Laverne hollered as the fighting rooster began to flog her, digging his crooked claws into her young skin. The rooster's wings whipped and flapped up and down and bits of feathers scattered wildly in the air. Angry rooster squawks and Laverne's yelps carried across the yard to Paul who had been on his way to the barn but was distracted by a tree limb hanging low. Paul was swinging on the tree limb when he heard his sister's screams.

With the snap of a twig, Paul let go of the branch and turned and ran as fast as he could to see what was wrong. Like a dancing boxer, he hopped back and forth, searching madly for the right angle to grab the rooster. Laverne was yelling and screaming and begging for help. Then, with both hands, Paul lunged for the rooster's neck and yanked him with full force off Laverne, swinging the rooster through the air and, at the same time, twisting his neck until it broke.

"That'll teach ya!" Paul declared with a mad jerk. The rooster went limp and flopped down dead. Like a rag doll, Paul threw the dead bird as hard as he could over the fence and out in a thicket where no one would know. It all happened so fast.

He walked over to Laverne who stood huddled and shaking from the rooster's scratches and scrapes on her back and arms. Thank goodness, only one claw mark on her arm was deep enough to bleed, and it wasn't bleeding very much. Laverne was more scared than she was hurt. To make matters worse, she had dropped the eggs on the ground and three of them had broken.

"Are ya all right?" Paul asked matter of factly. He didn't dare touch her to show his concern. That would be sissy. And Paul sure couldn't let his little sister see him soft or she'd tell and he'd never hear the end of it.

"Look at my back," she cried. "Am I okay?" She pulled at her plain cotton dress that her mother had made from a flour sack and which was already worn out. She had to wear it to school and was afraid it had been torn.

"Yer all right," Paul said with a quick glance. He turned and ran past the tree limb and onto the barn where he had to feed the pigs.

Laverne wiped her dirty, stained face and puckered her lower lip. She let a tear roll out of her little girl eyes after Paul was out of sight. Boy, if that rooster hadn't surprised her, she could have wrung its neck by herself. She was just as tough as Paul. Yes sir, she was as strong as her older brothers and sure enough, stronger than her younger ones. Who said girls were cowards? She could climb a tree, ride a horse, feed the stock, run, throw rocks, and do just about everything boys did. She was a real tomboy. Except, she had to help her mother all the time with the washing and cooking and taking care of all the boys.

Laverne bent down and picked up the two good eggs. She quickly buried the three broken ones under some dirt and grass and headed to the back door of the farmhouse. She was worried about what to tell her mother because every egg was important food to the family. It was hard to feed six kids on a dirt and red clay farm like theirs. Most folks were poor enough in this flat corner of southeast

Missouri. Their town was called Sank, what there was of it, but Laverne and her family lived out in the boonies.

She didn't know much about the Depression or World War II, or how people everywhere were trying to rebuild their lives and reline their pocketbooks. But, as a child, she did know her big family was extra poor. And she sure enough knew her mother would not be happy about Paul killing a good rooster or her breaking three fresh eggs. Laverne sighed and hoped no one would find out.

"Get them dishes on the table," Laverne's mother hollered from the back room where she was tending to one of the baby boys. Her mother's voice sounded irritable. With six rambunctious kids, it was no wonder her mother was tired before the day had even started, and she stayed sick and cranky most of the time from asthma or something. Laverne wasn't sure.

Laverne slammed the screen door to the three-room shack where she had been born, knowing there would be a pile of dishes to wash, dry, and put up after they ate breakfast, and then more than a dozen dirty diapers to scrub on the metal washboard and hang on the line. Laverne had to get all her chores done before she could leave for Cane Creek School, about a mile away, across the creek and down the gravel road.

She didn't mind walking to the one-room country school where all eight grades were together. Laverne had been taught by the same teacher, Mrs. Ola Francis, ever since the first grade, and she would graduate from the eighth grade when she was thirteen and maybe . . . just maybe, she could go to high school. She was a smart girl, and getting an education might be her ticket to a better life, out of the poorhouse and away from this hard farm work.

But, along with her impossible dream to fly like a bird, she knew getting a high school education was not likely.

Laverne's dad didn't want her to go to high school. He
told her no. She had to stay home and cook and wash and
keep house like women had always done. These were the
years after World War II when more and more females
across America were getting an education and going to
work in offices and factories. But men like Laverne's father could not see the value or reason why a woman
needed to be educated when all a woman did was have
babies and take care of kids and do housework. And one
other thing. No one could deny Laverne was a ripening
beauty, and her dad didn't like her around boys. There
were boys in high school.

"I hate them stinkin' ol' milk crocks!" Laverne mumbled to herself as she stomped across the kitchen floor. The
cream separator and milk jugs were waiting to be washed
after breakfast, and she hated washing them as much as
crawling under the house. They were big clay containers
used to keep sour milk for baking loaves of bread.

Laverne laid the good eggs on the counter top by the
dishpan and water bucket. She was thinking about all the
dishes and things she had to wash before she could leave
for school. Every single morning she had to wash and
scald all the pieces to that cream separator, the discs and
lids and paddles, and if she didn't get them washed, she'd
get a switching.

"What took sa long in the henhouse?" Laverne's
mother scolded her. Her mother stood in the doorway to
the backroom with a frown. Laverne's youngest brother
was in diapers, hanging onto his mother's neck and sad-
dled on her hip. The baby was whining, and Laverne's
two other little brothers were arguing and chasing each
other around the kitchen table. The older boys were still
in the barn. "Where's Paul?" Laverne's mother asked.
"You younguns' hurry up! And get them crocks cleaned up

or yer gonna get a lickin'.'" Her mother shouted over the whines and whoops of all the little boys. Laverne knew her mother was serious. Laverne had gotten plenty of switchings in her life, and now it was even worse because her mother made her go out back and cut the hickory stick herself. The last time Laverne got a whipping, she found a thicker and older hickory stick and hit herself on the legs to see how badly it hurt. Not too bad. She knew very well how those green hickory switches, thin and limber, cut like a razor.

Laverne rushed to dish up bowls of hot oats and pour the morning's milk. She was trying to hurry and get breakfast on the table, dodge her little brothers, keep her mother happy, and get all the chores done in time to go to school. Her ten-year-old mind was overloaded. There was much to do. She had to clear the table, wash and dry the dishes, scald the crocks, scrub the dozen dirty diapers, hang them on the line, hope no one found out about the dead rooster, and, and . . . Just then her foot caught on the leg of the old wooden table, she stumbled and spilled a churn of milk all over the linoleum floor.

Laverne swore out loud.

"What'd you say?" Her mother yelled at her through the doorway.

"Nothin' . . . I said 'Oh, shoot!' " Laverne stammered.

Her mother peeked into the kitchen and saw the fresh milk from their cow all over the floor. She scowled, "Can't you do nothin' right? Yer the clumsiest kid I ever saw. Get that mess cleaned up right now or I'm gonna whip the tar outta you!"

Laverne swallowed her hurt and anger like she had done as far back as she could remember. It wasn't her fault. She was trying so hard. Why couldn't her mother see? It wasn't her fault there were six hungry kids, or they were so poor, or that her mother was sick, and her dad stayed worked up and in a mean mood all the time over bad crops and no money.

Laverne swore under her breath again. She liked saying that word because her older brothers said that word and plenty more swear words when they played away from the house or behind the barn, *so why couldn't she?*

"Just ain't fair," she said, wishing she had not been born a girl. Sometimes, she wished she were a boy. Her brothers never got a switching from their mother for not washing dishes and diapers. They didn't get a tongue lashing when housework needed to be done or clothes needed washing. But she knew that wasn't really true. Her older brothers got worse whippings than she did and over the strangest things. She remembered not long ago her father jerked up the two older boys and gave them a terrible beating for sitting on a log after they had watered the cattle.

"Just ain't fair," Laverne fought back the tears.

       ❧ ❧ ❧

"Come on, Laverne!" Jessie yelled through the woods. "I think we're supposed to go this way." Jessie was Laverne's very best girlfriend, and they played together and stayed all night with each other whenever they could. This evening, they were on their way through the woods to a revival at Cane Creek Baptist Church. The little girls had planned to hitch a ride on the back of a horse-drawn wagon with Laverne's grandparents. They had planned to meet at the end of the lane, but for some reason, Laverne's grandparents didn't come by. Laverne was sure they had just missed them. If she and Jessie hurried, they could catch her grandparents on the road, up ahead.

So the two girls decided they would skip and walk and talk, and they could tell each other secrets on the way to the revival. It didn't matter that Laverne didn't know where the church was located because Jessie said she knew. Or, she thought she knew. The church was a mile or so down this road, across the swollen creek and through the woods. Laverne and Jessie were cleaned up, their hair combed, their new shoes wiped to a shine and besides, going to a revival was better than staying at home and fighting with the boys and doing chores.

Laverne and Jessie were about the same age so they told each other their deepest little-girl secrets. Laverne was happy. It was a great thrill to have a real live girl to talk to instead of a house full of boys. Laverne told Jessie about crawling under the house to gather eggs, the old rooster that jumped her, and how Paul wrung its neck and threw it in the bushes. She told about spilling the crock of milk and how angry her mother was over the accident.

She told Jessie one more secret. About Paul's friend who walked home with them one afternnoon last week and who was the only boy in school who had a bicycle. Laverne wanted to ride that boy's bicycle as much as anything she'd ever wanted to do.

"Humph!" Laverne said, "he said I could ride his bike . . . if I'd kiss him." Laverne snickered as she told Jessie what had happened.

"Did ya kiss him?" Jessie squealed as she hopped over a puddle of muddy water. It had come a heavy rain earlier that day so the ground was soft and deep pools of water stood in the gravel road tempting them to wade through instead of go around.

"Nope. I'd rather kiss a toad than him."

"Did ya ride his bike?"

"Yep."

"How did ya?" Jessie asked with widening eyes. "Without havin' to kiss him?"

Laverne shrugged her shoulders. "I told him I'd kiss him after I got to ride."

"Did ya kiss him or didn't ya?" Jessie asked impatiently.

"I took his bike and rode off to the bottom of the big hill and when he got there, he said he wanted his kiss."

Jessie's eyes twinkled. "Oh-h-h."

"I didn't want ta loose my breath pushin' that bike up the hill, so I dropped it and ran off, lickety split, over the hill," Laverne giggled. "And he had to push the bike up the hill and couldn't catch me to get his kiss."

Both little girls tee-heed and burst with laughter as they skipped down the lonely road. When they had started walking, the girls felt confident because they were following a pair of wagon tracks in the muddy, rocky road. They were sure the ruts were from Laverne's grandparent's wagon. But then, the tracks disappeared.

"Must be this way!" Jessie pointed. There was a wide path off to the right and through the woods.

All of a sudden, Laverne felt uneasy. It was getting late in the evening and the trail through the trees looked spooky. Long shadows draped across the path like black ribbons. Bushes were thick and blocked the way in places. Tree limbs reached down like big arms trying to grab them. Laverne had never been through these woods and certainly had never been to Cane Creek Baptist Church or to a revival before. She wasn't allowed to go many places, except to school and sometimes to visit relatives or Jessie's house.

She wasn't sure this was the thing to do. Maybe they should turn around and go home. She didn't go to church anyway. At Laverne's house, whenever anyone mentioned going to church, there was always a fuss and fight. Although her mother was raised a Methodist, her mother didn't read the Bible or pray where Laverne's father could see. Her father would sit on the front porch on Sunday mornings and grumble.

"Look at them fools drivin' over this rough gravel road and tearin' up their vehicles goin' to church!" he would say. He thought people and horses ought to rest on Sundays, or if anyone who could afford a car in such hard times, they sure enough needed their heads examined to drive over these back roads.

It was getting darker. Laverne and Jessie couldn't see all the mud holes and stumps along the wooded path. Almost twilight, the first evening star blinked down at them from the sky but the little girls didn't notice as they walked faster and faster. There was no breeze, just still air that was damp and thick with humidity. It felt swampy and creepy. Frogs and crickets began to wake up the quiet forest, and Laverne got more worried with each step. A hoot owl sat watching from a tree.

"Hoo-o-o . . . Hoo-o-o!"

Laverne jumped. "Oh! That scared me."

"Ah-h-h, nothin' but a ol' owl," Jessie said. She tried to sound brave.

"Oh no!" Laverne cried. The evening shadows were so long she had not seen the hole and had stepped in a big mud puddle, burying her new white shoes. It had taken her months to earn enough money, bottle feeding baby lambs the ewes wouldn't nurse, to buy the shoes out of a Sears and Roebuck catalog. They were the best and newest pair of shoes she'd ever had.

"I'm really gonna get a switchin' now," Laverne moaned. She pulled her feet up and out of the murky mud. She took a worried breath and fought back tears. No matter what she did, it seemed like she was always getting into trouble and always getting a switching. Laverne grabbed some big leaves and a bushy stick and wiped the white shoes as clean as she could in the dusk light. She yanked off her socks and decided to walk the rest of the way barefoot, that is, if they could find their way to church.

"We're lost! Ain't we, Jessie?" Laverne accused.

"We ain't either," Jessie said back.

"How do ya know?"

"Just do."

"You don't know the way!" Laverne snapped at her friend.

"Do too!"

Both girls were scared and on the verge of a squabble. There was fear and tension in their words to each other. Laverne knew the truth. Jessie didn't know the way to the church anymore than she did, but Jessie wouldn't dare admit it. The woods were almost black by now. It was a moody land of sounds that seemed to get louder and louder. There were singing katydids, croaking frogs, rustling leaves, hoots from owls, bushes that brushed against them, and imaginary monsters everywhere. Quietly and carefully they walked ahead, step by step through the dark. Without saying a word, Laverne and Jessie reached for each other's hands.

"We gotta be gettin' close," Laverne whispered.

"Cain't be far," Jessie said.

Just as they rounded an overgrown turn in the woods, going in a new direction, they thought they saw something flickering up ahead. Although their eyes were adjusted to the dark, they still weren't sure. Maybe it was a patch of lightning bugs. Squeezing their hands together, they crept closer. Laverne felt stickers under her bare feet.

Tiptoeing, the little girls looked over a low thicket of vines and pulled back a bush in order to see through.

"Hey, looky there!" Laverne pointed through the dark.

Across an open grassy field, the little girls could see the outline of a building against the background of a black forest and an ashen sky. There stood the small, one room, wooden Baptist church with dim burnt-orange lights shining through each of the narrow windows. The quivering lights were from kerosene lamps hanging on the walls inside the church. With deep sighs of relief, Laverne and Jessie grinned in the dark.

"See," Jessie smarted. "I told ya I knew the way."

"Humph!" Laverne added, ignoring Jessie's claim. "Come on, let's see if my grandparents' team and wagon are here."

Laverne hurriedly pulled on her socks and wet shoes so she could jump the briar thicket and get over into the grassy field. The girls whispered and giggled and felt like themselves again. They had found the way. They darted across the soggy dark field and when they got closer to the church, they could hear singing voices through the open windows that were propped up with sticks. Laverne had never heard such beautiful music before and it pulled at her heart like a magnet.

"What's that?" Laverne whispered.

"Ain't you never heard church singin' before?" Jessie asked.

"Nope," Laverne said. Jessie didn't know this was Laverne's first time to be away from home to go to church.

The girls crept next to the church windows, stretched their necks as high as they could and peeked inside. Laverne's mouth dropped open and her grey eyes widened. In the kerosene light, she could see about thirty people sitting on long wooden benches holding books in one hand and fanning themselves with a wide paper fan with the other. They weren't reading stories. They were singing songs. A lady was playing an old out-of-tune piano up front. All ages of people were there.

"Come on. Let's go inside." Jessie pulled at Laverne.

Laverne swallowed hard. She didn't see her grandparents inside, and she didn't know any of these people. The girls held hands as they crouched down and moved silently around the building to the front of the church where all the horses and wagons were parked. Laverne squinted her eyes in the dark but still did not see a familiar wagon. Her grandparents weren't here and suddenly, Laverne felt like running away. What now? In her ten-year-old mind, she could see angry parents and a green hickory switch. This church and all these people were so different from anything she had known or experienced. She wanted to go home.

Like frightened mice, the two little girls in their mud-soaked shoes and bashful eyes sneaked in the heavy door of the church. The wooden door was swollen because of the rain and humidity. The pews and all the congregation inside the one-room building faced the opposite direction and away from the door. Laverne and Jessie quietly moved on their tiptoes toward the back bench, hoping no one would turn around and notice them. Laverne's heart pounded so fast and loud she was sure everyone could hear it. With each step she took, the plank floor creaked and sounded like a groan for help. On the third step, a handful of older people turned and looked at the pair of girls and shy Laverne thought she was going to faint from embarrassment.

A farmer dressed in overalls stood up front and told the congregation to turn to page 117 in their hymn book.

Laverne and Jessie sank down on the back pew with a relieved sigh, as if they had made a home run in a baseball game. People were busy turning the pages of their hymn books and no longer looking at the two girls. Going to church was the scariest thing Laverne had ever done in her young life. She looked over at Jessie who was flipping pages in the song book. Jessie pushed a yellowed and tattered hymn book under Laverne's face and ran her finger across the lines to show Laverne the right verse. Laverne had never sung out of a hymn book before.

"Start singin' here," Jessie whispered.

Laverne looked at the page and the words. Hard working farmers began to sing in deep tones and old women in cotton dresses began to sing in high squeaky voices and aggravated young mothers sang in spurts while they twisted ears and thumped the heads of their squiriming children to make them stand still. The room full of singing voices sounded warm and earthy, but heavenly at the same time. The music filled the church house and went out the open windows into the quiet, country night. Kerosene lanterns flickered across the church casting soft shadows. Laverne opened her mouth and began to sing the words.

> Precious Lord, take my hand,
> Lead me on, let me stand,
> I am tired, I am weak, I am worn . . .
> Thru the storm, thru the night,
> Lead me on to the Light,
> Take my hand, Precious Lord,
> Lead me home . . .

With each word Laverne sang, it felt like a year of time passed in her life. She thought the song had been written for her. She'd never heard the song before, but yes . . . Just like the words she was singing, she was tired, she was worn, and she felt the troubles of the world on her ten-year-old shoulders. In a sudden wave of sadness, she felt heavy and like an old woman. All she had ever known was being poor and working hard work on a red dirt farm, and getting scolded and switched and punished. Was there really a Precious Lord in Heaven who would love her? Hold her hand? The words to the song began to pierce deep within, and she couldn't control the stirring she felt.

Nervous and uneasy, she held her breath so no one, not even Jessie, could see what she was feeling or thinking. Laverne was afraid to look up or turn her head. She shifted her weight from one foot to the other and looked down at her soiled Sears and Roebuck shoes. She thought if she stood totally still, that whatever was waking up inside of her would go back to sleep. What was happening? She couldn't wait until the song was over so she could sit down. The song continued.

> When my way grows drear,
> Precious Lord linger near
> When my life is almost gone,
> Hear my cry, hear my call
> Hold my hand lest I fall,
> Take my hand, Precious Lord
> Lead me home . . .

Laverne struggled to understand her emotions but couldn't. In a simple way, all she could understand about her feelings was that she felt lost and wanted someone to take her hand. She wanted to be loved and feel good inside. She had no way of knowing how this country church meeting or this hymn would change the rest of her life. She was only a child. And in this young and tender moment, she felt a divine pull to trust in God. Little Laverne would never be the same again.

❧ ❧ ❧

Three summers passed. Laverne was baptized in the cold waters of Cane Creek by a Baptist preacher with a wooden leg who walked with a limp. His name was Bill Elledge, and he was a relative on her father's side of the family. The dozen people to be baptized that day stood on the creek bank and sang hymns and had a prayer. Then, they held hands and walked way out into the water until they were waist deep. Laverne's cotton dress floated around her like a balloon. The preacher had one hand on the back of her head and lifted his other hand toward heaven and said he was baptizing Laverne in the name of the Father, the Son, and the Holy Ghost. He placed a white handkerchief over Laverne's mouth and dipped her backwards until her head went completely under the water. When Laverne came up out of the creek, the preacher quoted a scripture and said her baptism symbolized being raised from the dead like Jesus Christ. Now she was meant to walk in a new life.

Laverne hoped this new life meant she wouldn't have to work so hard and that she could go to high school. Laverne's father had softened on some of his religious opinions because he had recently started going to church himself, so he gave Laverne permission to attend youth meetings and church on Sundays, but that was enough. Laverne could not go to high school. Although she had graduated from the eighth grade, just as she feared, she had to stay home and cook, clean, haul water up the hill, and wash clothes for the five boys in the family.

Each weekday morning, Laverne stood at the kitchen window scrubbing the stinking milk crocks and breakfast dishes in a big metal pan. She watched for the yellow school bus with an ache inside and whenever she missed seeing the bus, she cried angry, hurt tears where no one could see. The bus would grind to a stop in front of the three-room farmhouse, and Laverne's older brothers, Paul and Orville, would hop aboard. They were allowed to go to high school but not pretty Laverne.

The bus was full of farm boys and girls, laughing and making friends and having fun. Paul had several high school buddies but one of his friends on the bus, Curtis Eaker, had noticed Laverne and had started smiling and waving to her each morning when the bus would stop. One spring morning, soon after the garden had been planted and vegetables were sprouting, the bus full of kids screeched to a loud stop on the country road in front of Laverne's house. She stood watching from the kitchen window. Curtis smiled and waved as usual, but this time, he threw a piece of paper out the window of the bus. Laverne saw him and wondered what it was.

As soon as the bus drove away, Laverne ran out the kitchen door, through the garden and next to the gravel road searching for the paper. She looked and looked but could not find anything. She wondered if she had imagined the whole thing. Day after day she hunted for the paper but found nothing. About two weeks later, Laverne and her mother were in the garden pulling fresh onions and picking lettuce when Laverne's eye caught the glare of something shiny. She spied a little yellow, Juicy Fruit gum wrapper. Her eyes lit up. She wondered how in the world a piece of gum could have gotten there. Chewing gum was a rare treat, and she never had gum except on very special occasions.

She grabbed for it, but quickly noticed there was no gum. While her mother had her back turned and was busy picking lettuce leaves, Laverne quietly opened the foil wrapper and on the inside it said, "April Fool!" Laverne's heart leaped because she realized this was the lost note from Curtis Eaker, the older boy on the school bus. It was true. He had thrown a piece of paper out the window and had actually written a note to her. Now, she would really watch for the school bus.

Morning after morning, she stood washing dishes in front of the kitchen window and waited for that brief moment when she would see Curtis smile and wave to her. The smiles and waves continued for weeks until one day, Curtis drove up the gravel road in a new car and stopped in front of her house. He had bought his first car and wanted to show it to her brother, Paul. Curtis had a part-time job and would soon be out of high school, and he needed a car to go to work and college.

On that morning, Laverne had been chasing a chicken around the yard. Besides gathering eggs, washing clothes and dishes, it was her job to catch and kill the chickens to cook for dinner. Today, she was going to cook a big pot of chicken and dumplings. Laverne had stretched the banny hen's neck out and had raised her arm up in the air, ready to come down with a sharp blade and chop the chicken's head off when Curtis walked up.

"Here. Don't do that," he smiled. "Let me wring its neck. My grandmother does it all the time."

"I don't know how to do that," Laverne said. She liked his warm smile up close as well as from the kitchen window. And he seemed very kind as he stood tall and handsome beside her. Something about this boy made her feel different. Suddenly she became aware she was a girl and not just someone's sister.

"I can wring its neck," Curtis said looking down into her pretty grey eyes.

Curtis bravely took the flopping chicken from Laverne and squeezed it around the neck. With strong hands, he swung the chicken around in a circle and through the air. He cranked and cranked and cranked until he thought he had broken the hen's neck. With certainty, he threw the chicken down on the ground for dead. With another handsome smile, he turned and walked back to his car and drove away.

Meanwhile, the banny hen choaked and clucked a weak cluck, then hopped up and ran off. Laverne had to chase the chicken again and kill it herself, but she decided that this boy, Curtis Eaker, was worth killing a chicken for—twice. She grinned to herself and knew she liked this boy. Yes sir, she liked him a lot.

ะ. ะ. ะ.

Months and months passed and Laverne didn't see Curtis again. He was five years older than she and had graduated from high school and was gone away to college. Laverne figured the tall boy with the warm smile forgot her since she was just a young, backward farm girl. Life in the boonies stayed the same. Everyday, it was hauling water, cooking giant pots of beans and potatoes for all the boys, and washing clothes, feeding chickens, pigs, lambs, and working in the garden. The days were long and the harder Laverne worked, the sadder she felt. She couldn't figure out why, all of a sudden, she was clumsy and awkward. She kept dropping things and bumping into furniture and walking into door facings. She broke two dishes one morning after breakfast which made her mother very angry.

"What's wrong with you today?" her mother scolded, crawling all over Laverne.

Laverne wasn't sure what was wrong. In her mind, there were a lot of things troubling her but she didn't know how to fix them. She was fifteen years old, all grown up in her physical appearance, but still socially be-hind and shy because she could not go to high school. In some ways, she felt like an outcast. She felt dumb and inferior to the other boys and girls she knew who were getting an education and who would one day receive a high school diploma. *What is wrong with me?* she asked herself. Maybe she was lonesome. Living far out in the country and under her father's tight rule, her only contact with other teenagers was at church or youth meetings. She attended church, revivals, or any religious gathering as often as she could to be with girls and boys her own age, and it wasn't long until another boy took a shine to pretty Laverne. His name was Pooch. Although Laverne's father would not allow her to date this boy or any other boy, all the kids in the youth group secretly knew Pooch and La-verne were "going together" because Laverne was wearing Pooch's wrist watch.

One night Laverne went to church with her older brother Paul and his girlfriend. All the teenagers, includ-ing Pooch, would be at the youth meeting, and Laverne looked forward to getting away from the farm. To Laverne's surprise, a new part-time preacher showed up. *We'll I'll be . . .* thought Laverne. He was a recent college graduate who worked as a school teacher and part-time preacher. He was Paul's friend from the school bus. It was Curtis Eaker again. He had grown up and looked like a young man instead of a boy. Laverne watched him out of the corner of her eye and hoped he would speak to her. *Did he remember smiling at her? Did he remember the note? Did he know she was going with Pooch?*

After the singing and shouts of praise-the-Lord and a fiery sermon, a final prayer was spoken, and everyone felt their souls had been washed and were ready to go home. Pooch grinned at Laverne and told her goodbye in the front yard of the church because he was not allowed to take her home. On that night, Curtis offered to drive Paul and Paul's girlfriend home from church, and of course, it was all right for Laverne to ride back home with them because she was with her older brother.

Curtis pulled his car to the side of the empty gravel road near Laverne's farmhouse and stopped. Paul and his girlfriend began smooching in the back seat. Laverne sat still. She could hear Paul and his girlfriend whispering and cuddling in the back of the car. It was a star lit night. Crickets and frogs sang in the background.

Curtis looked over at pretty Laverne next to him in the front seat. She blinked her big grey eyes. Curtis carefully and slowly raised his right arm and placed it around her shoulder and pulled Laverne's girlish face close to his. He planted a quiet kiss on her lips. It was sweet and tender, more so than anything Laverne had ever felt.

"When you get through going with Pooch, you let me know," Curtis whispered.

Her heart was pounding and she felt a blush go up her neck and across her cheeks. She was sure Curtis could see her red face in the dark. Right then, Laverne lifted her arm and pulled off the wrist watch.

"I'm through," she said.

       ẽ   ẽ   ẽ

It was a humid hot Sunday in the spring of 1949, and Laverne was not quite sixteen years old. She sat in the steamy church pew, fanning herself and wiping her forehead, anxious for the sermon to end. All she could think about was that she had to have her father's permission in order to get married to the preacher, Curtis Eaker. Laverne was frightened to ask him.

"Let's not tell anyone. Let's run away and get married," Laverne pleaded.

"No, we're going to do this right," Curtis told her. Being level-headed as well as a preacher, it was important to Curtis that their marriage be proper.

After the church service that day, it worked out for Curtis and Laverne to ride home with her father. With just the three of them in the car, Curtis knew the moment was right.

"What do you think about Laverne and me getting married?" Curtis asked. His question came by surprise.

Laverne's father became stone silent. He never said a word. He turned his head away and looked out the car window as they drove down the narrow dirt road through the countryside on their way to his three-room farmhouse. A hot breeze came through the rolled-down windows on the car and made the silence seem like eternity. Plowed fields, woods, and fence rows loaded with honeysuckle vines were an everyday part of the landscape as well as grazing cows and horses. They passed an open field where a horse was munching on grass.

"Look at that horse," Laverne's father finally said.

The three of them rode in more silence. Laverne thought her heart would pop open if something didn't happen soon.

At long last, Laverne's father sighed, "I know there's no use tryin' to talk you kids outta this." He seemed resigned and did not make a fuss about their plans to marry. He agreed to sign the necessary legal papers since Laverne was under age. Curtis was already twenty-one.

A few days passed, and then on a sweltering, hot, sticky morning, Curtis picked up Laverne in his 1938 maroon Chevrolet. Six people loaded in the car. Although it was still early, the car was a human oven even with the windows rolled down. Laverne's father and Curtis's father came along as well as Paul and his girlfriend, Bessie. Today was the day. Curtis and Laverne were on their way to the next town to get married. Laverne's father could sign for her while Paul and Bessie stood as witnesses.

The six of them had not been in the car long and weren't very far down the two-lane highway when Curtis's car had a flat tire. The rising sun was bright and draining. The men changed the flat tire and when everyone squeezed back inside the Chevrolet, they journeyed on to find a justice of the peace. The courthouse in the first town was closed, so Curtis kept driving. They stopped in a second town. Good. The courthouse was open. After finding the right room and filling out several legal papers, the clerk asked Laverne her age. When Laverne explained she was fifteen years old but her father was here to sign, the clerk shook her head and said she was sorry because their county had just changed the law. Curtis and Laverne couldn't get married in this town.

Once more, the six hot and tired people walked wearily to the car and climbed in. After sweating all day, changing a flat tire, eating bologna sandwiches on the side of the road for lunch, and trying to get married in three towns, they drove on to the town of Pocahontas, Arkansas, where the courthouse was open, the justice of the peace was at hand, and the legal papers were in order. When Laverne came to the question about her age, she decided she wasn't taking any more chances. They had driven almost one hundred miles and had overcome enough hurdles for the day. From early that morning when she left the farm in Sank, Missouri, to that afternoon in Pocahontas, Arkansas, Laverne aged quickly and went from being fifteen to eighteen years old.

Curtis stood nervous in a pin-striped suit, wet from perspiration, and Laverne stood shy but happy in her light blue taffeta dress with a wilted pink corsage. Paul and Bessie stood proud beside them as witnesses while both fathers silently watched and kept their thoughts to themselves. On May 6, 1949, the little farm girl from the backwoods became the preacher's country wife.

៚ ៚ ៚

January, 1990. Laverne Eaker and I sat side by side on the long pew in the hushed sanctuary of the United Methodist Church. The church bell tolled across the rural town of Stewardson, Illinois, letting all the townspeople and corn and wheat farmers know it was time to worship. Groups of men and women filed through the front and side doors from Sunday school classes and walked to their favorite place to sit during the 10:30 A.M. service. Young people and rosy faced children moved quietly down the thick red carpeted aisles to sit with their parents or friends. Soft voices and whispers hummed while the organist played "God of Grace and God of Glory." The organ sounded soothing and solid and filled the room with reverence. A shaft of easy light made its way through a tall, arched stained glass window and fell across half of the people.

Laverne pulled a new hymnal from the book shelf on the pew in front of us and opened to page three. She looked well dressed and sophisticated wearing a black suit, plum sweater, and richly colored neck scarf. She wore shiny black earrings that enhanced the sparkle in her clear grey eyes. Laverne's eyes were spunky. Her dark brown hair was short and curly, and it was hard for me to believe she was a fifty-four-year-old grandmother. Laverne's face was still pretty and vibrant and young. She looked over at me and grinned.

"I'm so glad you are here," Laverne giggled and squirmed, patting me on the knee. "I'm missing Curtis already."

Curtis was the pastor of this congregation and had been for several years. Now he was close to retirement. This church was his final pastorate after over forty years as a minister of the Gospel. He usually sat on the platform in front of the choir loft, but today he was on a jet plane headed for Israel on a special tour of the Holy Land with an ecumenical group of twenty ministers from different denominations as well as a Catholic priest and rabbi. There would be a guest speaker for this morning's church service.

From her seat, Laverne greeted and smiled and waved at dozens of people as they passed by. She reminded me of a teenager. It was obvious she knew everyone, and they knew her. Her lively spirit seemed to brighten each person as they exchanged hellos. Laverne reached over the pew in front of us and cooed into the chubby face of a six-month-old baby. The baby's eyes widened, and a smile as broad as the hymnbook crossed the infant's face. Laverne couldn't resist short goo-goo talk and quick kisses on the baby's plump cheek. She had a way with babies and children, and they seemed to be so absorbed in each other that the rest of us faded away. Laverne was merry as the serious organ music played on. She did not act solemn. I thought most ministers' wives were grave, sober, staid, and often long-faced. Not Laverne. She was playful and child-like and energetic, even in God's house.

"You still don't act like a preacher's wife," I joked under my breath.

Laverne threw her head back and tried to hold down her laughter.

"Come on, I need to run out to the foyer and check the attendance record," she said, motioning for me to follow.

I grabbed my purse and eased out of the pew behind Laverne. We still had a few minutes before the service would start.

"Good morning."

"How are you?"

"Very well, thank you."

"Good morning." People nodded and greeted each other, and Laverne spoke to everyone as they passed us on their way to the sanctuary. Then she cut her experienced eyes over at me.

"Yes, I've had people tell me for years that I don't act like a preacher's wife." Laverne lowered her voice, "Not long ago, I had a well-educated young woman talk to me because her husband, his name was Ron, was going into the ministry. This woman said she couldn't see herself as a preacher's wife. She was scared to death and didn't know what to do!"

"So, what did you say to her?" I asked.

"I said, 'Can you see yourself as Ron's wife?' And she answered 'yes, of course,' she had always been Ron's wife." Laverne checked her watch to see how much time we had left and hurried to tell the rest of the story. "Then, I flat out told her, 'okay, you are no different now. You be yourself. You do what is best for you and your husband and your children, and if the people in the church can't understand, then let them complain. You ignore it and be yourself.'"

Laverne flipped the pages in the record book and looked back at me. Another couple walked by us and when they opened the door to the sanctuary, the organ music was now joined by the piano player preparing the congregation for the service. When the door shut, she continued.

"And I told the woman the same goes for your children. Church people expect your kids to be a little above everybody else's." All of a sudden, Laverne changed. I could feel righteous anger in the tone of her voice. Laverne and Curtis's three children were now in their mid and late thirties, married and had families of their own, but back in the 1960s, Mike, Alan, and Beth had gone through the stigma of being "preacher's kids." They were expected to be more saintly, closer to perfect, and to have fewer problems in life.

With fire, Laverne added, "Preacher's kids are as human as the church members' kids or anybody else's. They face the same world. They might take a drink of beer, puff on a cigarette, swear, get pregnant, get divorced, or just get into messes like other people do," Laverne quipped. "You can't push salvation or right living on anybody, even your own kids. The best way to get through to people is to let them see how you act."

Laverne looked down at her watch and motioned it was almost time to go back into the sanctuary. She sighed and quickly finished her thoughts.

"It all goes back to pleasing God. You have to do what you believe the Lord wants you to do and not what other people expect because that will give you ulcers." Her eyes jumped at me. She jerked her head back and let go of a muffled laugh, "I know, cause I had three of them."

I looked at this woman. Laverne was real. There were no airs, no falsehoods, and no phony religious play acting with her. I had known her over thirty years, from the time I was a young girl back in Missouri. Many of my childhood memories included Laverne because I attended the church where Curtis was pastor at that time, and spent many hours in their home and with their children who were close to my age. I remember their family was happy and laughed a lot. It was in 1962 when Curtis baptized me in Black River, and Laverne was like a second mother. She had guided me during those up and down teenage years when I was soaking up the meaning of life and what was important.

I watched her finish checking the record book and found it hard to believe this woman had come from such poor, uneducated, and humble beginnings. She looked so smart and stylish and had gobs of common sense. Then I remembered stories from the Bible. Most of the people God used were from the bottom of the barrel: peasants like David the shepherd boy, farm girls like Ruth the grain gatherer, Moses who couldn't talk well, fishermen, hustlers, prostitutes, tax collectors, and cowards like Jonah. Shy, little Laverne from a dirt farm and three-room shack in the boonies was no problem to God.

To end forty years as a preacher's wife in this Illinois church full of people was evidence she had served well. She had nurtured souls and wrapped her arms around hundreds of hurting people over the years.

"But, there's something I wish I were better at doing," she frowned. A twinge of regret crossed her face. "I get so mad at myself for not writing notes and cards to older people who can't get out and who need to know someone cares, but I just don't like to write."

"Hey, not everyone likes to write," I answered in defense, not wanting her to feel inadequate. "I'd much rather know you were praying for me than writing me notes all the time," I teased.

"You can be sure that's done!"

"Why, I need so much prayer, you've probably got callouses on your knees."

"Yeah, I'm about prayed-out over you!" She laughed.

Laverne sensed I was thinking good thoughts about her. She closed the record book, reached for her purse and threw her other arm around my shoulder. Her grey eyes glistened with devotion and her feisty face turned serious for a moment.

She paused holding her feelings in check. "I love you, Barb, like a daughter." Then she gave me a quick squeeze and pulled me toward the door leading into the sanctuary.

She giggled, "Come on. Let's go show 'em how to sing!"

LAVERNE'S FAVORITE PIE: RHUBARB PIE

Of all the pies I've ever had, rhubarb is my favorite pie.

You pick and clean several stalks of rhubarb, wash them, and dice them up to make about two cups of rhubarb. And then you have to have a nine-inch pie pan lined with pie crust.

You put the rhubarb in there and sprinkle about a cup and a half to two cups of sugar, depending on how sweet you want it. And then about a tablespoon full of flour or cornstarch over the top of that to kind of thicken it so the juice doesn't boil out in the oven. Put another crust over the top and cook that at about 350 degrees, until the rhubarb is tender, about thirty-five to forty minutes.

It's real easy, and it's delicious.

I love it!

❧ ❧ ❧

Chapter Six

IDAHO'S FAIR LADY

IT WAS LATE MAY and the bluebirds seemed to sing louder, and rowdy kids behaved better, and the warm sunshine tempted adults to stop work early and go for a picnic. It was the kind of day that made grown-ups feel peppy and young and all was right with the world. Women were beginning to feel the urge. That yearly fever to wash curtains, dust corners, rearrange furniture, clean out cupboards and closets, and shine the house from top to bottom. Housewives everywhere opened windows for clean breezes to blow out the stale smells that had built up over the winter. The season for change had finally arrived in the tiny northwestern town of Filer, Idaho.

There weren't many streets in Filer, but there were several rows of modest wood-framed houses, a grade school, the high school, a bank, drug store, post office, and some churches. Down the short dusty streets, irrigation ditches would soon be flowing with precious water for newly tilled gardens and lawns, and flowers were already showing off colorful petals. Spring was here and some of the townspeople would make the trip to Snake River Canyon, a few miles out of town, to see the bountiful orchards of fruit trees covered in fragrant blossoms and noisy bees. The first cherry, peach, pear, and apple trees had been

149

planted in the deep canyon by early settlers forty to fifty years ago.

Men were in town. Cattle ranchers and potato and bean farmers passed each other on Filer's main street, walking briskly to the bank or drug store. They clicked the dust off their work boots and smiled more easily under their wide brim hats and farmer's caps. Their faces carried creases from working outdoors under big western skies and a bright sun. Today's crisp air helped them forget, briefly, about their money troubles and hope for better days ahead. These men wanted to forget how hard they had worked last summer and fall to make it through the lean and snowbound winter. Winters in Idaho could be mean and cold because freezing storms would blast down from Alaska and Canada and sweep across the northern Rocky Mountain range and dip down into the big valley that stretched across the southern portion of Idaho where Filer was located. The southern strip across the lower part of the state was known as Magic Valley.

Here the land was lush and green with cloudless skies and roaring rivers. Some of the deepest canyons in North America weaved their quiet and awesome way through the valley. Fossil beds and prehistoric secrets lay hushed in the rocks and steep canyons. This unspoiled beauty, along with the plentiful pheasant, goose, duck, deer, and other wildlife caused pioneers in the 1800s who were headed to the Northwest to stop and take a second look. Many stayed in southern Idaho and formed the town of Twin Falls and then scattered throughout the countryside, banding together in little towns like Filer. Filer was seven miles from Twin Falls.

Although the Oregon Trail would have taken pioneers further north and west to Oregon, a number of early settlers saw the black dirt and thought it would be good soil to farm. Years later with the growth of agricultural trade and newspapers, the rest of America learned southern Idaho had the most fertile land anywhere in North America because it was loaded with volcanic ash and rock. Now, Magic Valley was dotted with farmhouses, rustic barns, grassy pastures with a few haystacks left over from the winter, and irrigated fields to be planted in wheat, beans, potatoes, and seed crops.

But it wasn't the rich, dark dirt that had put new creases in the faces of the local farmers and cattlemen. The men in Filer as well as people across the United States were worried about money. It was 1929 and businesses were closing, people were losing their jobs, and mortgages were being foreclosed. They called it the Great Depression, and it had hit faraway states like Idaho and tiny towns no one had ever heard of before, like Filer. At least with spring popping-out, farmers and ranchers were thinking about plowing new dirt and planting their crops, counting newborn calves, and finding ways to make money to pay bills and hang onto their land. Things would get better. President Herbert Hoover said prosperity was just around the corner.

A few blocks off the main street in Filer, Mrs. Dillingham was busy with her spring cleaning as the sun pushed higher toward noon. She dusted the grand piano, swept the thick Oriental carpets, and checked exquisite vases and glassware for smudges that needed to be cleaned. It was time to wipe dust from everything, and she must remember the wooden frames around the oil paintings. Mrs. Dillingham was a thin and well mannered woman who took great pride in keeping her nicely furnished home spotless and orderly. Hers was one of the finest, if not the finest, house in Filer, and the money worries from the Great Depression seemed to have passed over the

Dillingham home. She and her husband were prominent and respected citizens of Filer and considered well-to-do. Mr. Dillingham was the town pharmacist and had been since 1920. He owned the only drug store, better known as The Modern Drug Shop, while Mrs. Dillingham stayed busy as a happy homemaker with Methodist church meetings and their one child, pretty Lucy Adele. Lucy Adele was nine years old and in the third grade. She was their lovely daughter and joy in life. She had brown sparkly hair, pastel blue eyes, and an ivory complexion that made her look like a fragile porcelain doll. She was sensitive and shy with a gentle streak to her personality. Being an only child, she was not much of a talker. While other children her age were slurping watermelons, riding bicycles, and playing basketball, Lucy Adele was learning social graces and proper table settings. And, there were the piano, ballet, and violin lessons too.

"Lucy Adele—Lucy Adele," Mrs. Dillingham sang from the doorway. "Come on, it's time for lunch." There would be fresh soup and toasted bacon and tomato sandwiches with crisp lettuce to eat. Mrs. Dillingham's voice was kind and as clear as a bell. There was no sign in Mrs. Dillingham's manner of the rough economic times that made most folks bitter and deprived, nothing to suggest there was a depression except for Lucy Adele's young playmate who lived across the street. Her name was Miriam. Mrs. Dillingham kindly suggested Miriam run and play while Lucy Adele had lunch.

"Can Lucy Adele play after she eats?" Miriam asked.

"Yes, dear," Mrs. Dillingham smiled. "After she practices her piano lessons." Mrs. Dillingham was gracious and careful not to make Miriam feel uncomfortable, but it was lunch time, and Lucy Adele had to practice the piano. It was not

Lucy Adele's nature to cross her mother, so she quietly obeyed and playtime would have to wait until later.

Lucy Adele looked longingly at Miriam who ran down the street, skipping and hopping, and then Miriam jumped the irrigation ditch to get home to her tiny house. Miriam was a fun and smart girl with blonde hair that didn't get combed too often, and whose fingernails were clogged with dirt and who was barefoot a lot of the time. Lucy Adele and Miriam attended the same elementary school and had been playmates since the first grade. Over the past three years, they had jumped rope, played jacks, hopscotch, ball-bouncing, swinging, and straddled the irrigation ditches.

It didn't matter to Lucy Adele that Miriam's family was very poor, or that they lived from hand-to-mouth because Lucy Adele loved the whole family. Miriam's mother was a tired widow woman who worked long hours to earn money, doing ironing and house cleaning while Miriam's brothers and sisters scraped up odd jobs to buy food for the large family of six children. Along with other cleaning jobs, Miriam's mother would clean house for Mrs. Dillingham. Whenever Lucy Adele outgrew her dresses or didn't wear them, Mrs. Dillingham would give them to Miriam. In 1929, there were no widow's pensions, or social security, no public welfare or other government programs to help poverty stricken families. Help had to come from friends, neighbors, and the local church.

Lucy Adele was not embarrassed that her best friend lived in a cracker box house with cheap cabbage rose linoleum and tacky wicker furniture. In fact, Lucy Adele secretly wished she had been as lucky as Miriam—to grow up in a big family with six kids and to have all those brothers and sisters to play, fight, and eat with, and to feel like she was a part of a festive bunch. If she were like

Miriam, then she would have people near her own age to laugh with, talk to, share games, and just be together. Miriam and her needy family were the substitute brothers and sisters Lucy Adele wished for, but would never have.

No one suspected the truth because Lucy Adele was too quiet and modest and never spoke out of turn. In spite of a fancy bedroom filled with enamelled pink furniture and a rocking chair to match and bay window to sit in and read *Child Life* magazines, there were many times Lucy Adele felt lonely. All of her piano, ballet, violin lessons, and pretty clothes didn't take away the aloneness she often felt. Her world was isolated. She had always kept these deep feelings to herself because there was no one to tell. Even her best friend, Miriam, wouldn't understand because Miriam thought Lucy Adele was a golden princess who lived in a castle. Their lives were very different.

🙞 🙞 🙞

"It's time to go," Mr. Dillingham announced. He was packing the family car with luggage and would be driving his wife and Lucy Adele to the train station in Shoshone, Idaho, for them to catch the next passenger train into Denver, Colorado and then on to Kansas.

"Let me run and tell Miriam goodbye," Lucy Adele cried as she dashed out the front door and across the powdery-dirt street to Miriam's plain little house. She would not see Miriam until mid-summer and must tell her goodbye.

"Hurry!" Mrs. Dillingham called after Lucy Adele.

Lucy Adele was the most excited she had been all year. There was a smile across her creamy face as long as the violin she played. Her lovely, soft-colored blue eyes sparkled. Today, she and her mother were leaving on their yearly pilgrimage back to see Lucy Adele's grandparents who lived in a grand two-story house outside their town of Pomona, Kansas. Her grandparents' house faced the Ozarks. It was a long trip, even by modern train.

Lucy Adele was anxious to tell Miriam about the gobs of fireworks that would be set off on the Fourth of July back in Kansas. All her cousins would be there. She must tell Miriam how she would ride a horse, and that while she was in Kansas, she could go anyplace she wanted on a bicycle. What fun. What freedom. Of course, she would tell Miriam how much she would miss her. Lucy Adele pounded on the front door of the little house. She was ready to explode with excitement.

Her happy smile faded when no one came to answer the loud knocks that shook the thin walls. Everyone was gone. They all must be working, and she had missed saying goodbye to Miriam. Lucy Adele turned, long faced, and strolled back across the deserted street where her parents were waiting in the car. There was no time left to write Miriam a note or a letter, but she remembered she had written a poem in Miriam's notebook earlier in the year, and hopefully, Miriam would read it while Lucy Adele was back in Kansas: "I like coffee, I like tea, I like you, if you like me. Your best playmate, Lucy Adele."

Mr. and Mrs. Dillingham smiled through the car window at their daughter. There was compassion and understanding on their adult faces. They knew how much Lucy Adele loved Miriam, but they also knew there were people, like Miriam and her widowed mother, who had more hardships to face in life than others. Mr. and Mrs. Dillingham looked at Lucy Adele's disappointed face and wished they could wave a magic wand and make the troubles of Miriam's family go away. They wished they had the answers to why suffering and dark days fell on some families and not others. They wished they could change things and make everyone in their town prosperous, but that wasn't how the real world worked.

Mrs. Dillingham assured Lucy Adele the time would pass quickly, and she'd see Miriam before she knew it.

"When we get to Denver, we'll have several hours until our train arrives, so we'll go shopping, or take a taxi and go see a movie," Mrs. Dillingham said soothingly. She wanted to cheer her daughter.

Mr. Dillingham pulled the car away from their handsome home and drove down Main Street, passing rows of poplar trees and hardwoods and yards full of flowers to get to the highway. Lucy Adele looked back at Miriam's humble house as they rounded the corner and out of sight. There weren't many cars on the two-lane highway because gasoline was hard to get.

Mr. Dillingham would not be going with his wife and daughter on the trip back to Kansas because he had to stay in Filer and keep the drug store open. Lucy Adele and her mother had made this trip every year since 1920, the year Lucy Adele was born, and they would be gone for six weeks. Mr. Dillingham would miss them, yet, he enjoyed seeing his wife and daughter excited, and traveling in their fancy dresses and hats to match. Lucy Adele also wore new colored anklets and slippers. Mr. Dillingham smiled with approval.

"Don't forget, you'll be on the train for two nights and there's lots to see between here and Kansas." Mr. Dillingham said with a grin.

"And, we'll have consommé in the diner car," Mrs. Dillingham added. "Remember those elegant meals and the lovely white linen napkins?"

"Yes, Mother," Lucy answered.

"Remember the tables in the dining car are lined with silver, and how the waiters place the napkins in our laps?"

"Yes, Mother."

Lucy Adele appreciated her parents efforts to soften the disappointment over not saying goodbye to Miriam. She knew they were trying to change her mood and get her mind back on the trip. Lucy Adele sighed. She adjusted her pristine hat and straightened the full skirt on her dress as she sat in the back seat of the car. She crossed her legs and noticed a bit of dirt on her colored anklets. She didn't care. Lucy Adele looked out the car window as her father drove down the narrow highway and talked with her mother about last minute details. Lucy Adele wondered where Miriam had gone.

Someday, she was going to get up the courage to tell Miriam how much she missed her when she went back to Kansas every summer, how special their friendship was, how she wanted to be like Miriam and live in a big family, how she dreamed of having five or six kids of her own, how they would call her "Mama" instead of "Mother," and . . .

"Oh, well." She took a deep breath. Today, Lucy Adele just wished she could have told Miriam goodbye and what a tomboy she would be back in Kansas.

ॐ ॐ ॐ

The three of us, Lucy Adele, her husband of forty-eight years, Jack Ramsey, and I, were sitting in front of the fireplace in their cozy den on Yakima Street remembering how we met years ago. It was a bright but blustery early spring day in Filer and perfect for conversation and reflecting on shared memories in front of a toasty fire. Our friendship dated back to 1978 when I was walking across America and writing and taking photographs for *National Geographic Magazine*. Lucy Adele and Jack Ramsey had

graciously opened their home and made me feel like part
of their family at that time.

Not much about the house had changed in the twelve
years since I had been here. The den was still the same
comfortable and lively room laden with original artwork
and lined with bookshelves on one side of the fireplace
filled with Colorado and New Mexico pottery, candles,
Indian relics, and books. On the other side of the carpeted
room, there sat the same small breakfast table and brown
washer and dryer. Today, the breakfast table was topped
with baskets of blooming primroses in hot yellow, violet,
and neon pink colors that brought even more cheer to the
already colorful house. Crystal droplets hung in one window, catching the Idaho sunlight and making rainbows
across the floor. It felt time had stood still and it was only
yesterday that I had been here.

Lucy Adele, now seventy years old and with white
curly hair, was snuggled in a big recliner chair beside the
wide picture window and under the same floor lamp working on the most spectacular needlepoint rug I had ever
seen. It was 3' by 5'. Her eyes had stayed brilliant blue
and her face ivory white. The porcelain beauty from childhood, as well as from twelve years ago, had lasted and her
smile was as quick as ever. It was only her instant wit and
one-liners that had become more noticable.

She kept one leg curled up underneath her as she
pulled the needle back and forth through the heavy fabric
with the skill of a master artisan. Each stitch was deliber-
ate and time consuming. Projects took hours and hours
and sometimes months, even a year to finish. I watched
her while the logs on the fire popped and the rainbow of
colors from the sunlit crystals in the window danced
across the room. It was a mellow moment as Lucy Adele,

Jack, and I sat in silence, enjoying the sleepy fire and each other's friendship.

Then a thought hit me.

"I need to hang some of those crystal droplets in my kitchen window. My kids would love to watch all of the colors," I said, making small talk. We had already spent hours catching up on the news from Tennessee and Idaho and the three of us were taking a little break from our long dialogue. Little snippets of conversation were all that was needed.

Lucy shook her head back and forth and breathed a heavy sigh. She asked me if I had heard about the Crystal Movement.

"The what?" I asked.

"I just can't understand . . ." Lucy Adele pondered as she pushed the needle up and down through the fabric. "Haven't you heard how people are wearing crystal necklaces and rubbing crystals to connect with a higher force?"

"Are you kidding?" I asked.

"Nope," Lucy Adele said. "Barbara, where have you been?"

"With my nose in Rebekah's fifth grade homework!" I laughed.

"Wel-l-l-l" she sang, "it's pretty big stuff, all that's going around, like 'channeling' and 'crystals.' People are grabbing the newest thing that comes along. They feel like they have to explore everything." She never looked up from her needlework. The fire flickered and radiated waves of warmth. "And it's just so simple," she mumbled as an afterthought.

Jack was quiet, reading the newspaper and glancing over occasionally to watch the flames and see if it was time to throw on another log. With all of Lucy Adele's flair for art and sensitive temperment, Jack was steady as a rock. He was an anchor in the middle of Lucy Adele's river of creativity, always staid and easy-going. Jack Ramsey was a retired vice president of the Idaho First National Bank in Twin Falls after being a banker for thirty-eight years. While Jack read the paper and Lucy Adele worked on her needlepoint, my thoughts about the 'crystal movement' raced. *Oh, yes* . . . now I vaguely recalled an advertisement in a women's magazine about where to order crystal pendants and their secret powers. There were so many beliefs floating around, everything from the mystical spiritual experiences of Shirley McLaine to detailed horoscopes, psychic parties, reincarnation movements, cosmic forces, Renaissance Groups, New Age philosophies, and what was trendy to believe in and what wasn't. And, I thought how complicated and flaky the world was today compared to when I was a Missouri girl back in the 1960s searching for answers about life and death and the hereafter. But in the 1990s, there were dozens more movements to sort through and tempting spiritual choices people could make. I was curious what Lucy Adele meant.

"How is it so simple?" I finally asked, shifting my weight in the easy chair where I sat in front of the fire. I wanted to hear her answer because I had three young children to think about and give a solid religious foundation to.

Lucy Adele Dillingham Ramsey was no longer the shy golden princess she had been in her childhood. She was no longer afraid to share her thoughts or feelings or to speak frankly. She had become an articulate and stately woman with a college degree in Home Economics, married forty-eight years, the mother of five children (four sons and a daughter), a Sunday school teacher in the Methodist church, a leader in Filer affairs as well as a volunteer for school and scout projects, widely travelled, and more. The many years of her life had led Lucy Adlele into being an outgoing and confident person.

She did not hesitate to answer, "People will try everything." She looked over at me with translucent blue eyes that always said more than what she allowed to come out of her mouth. Then she said, "Why don't people try what's in the Bible? Just believe in God!"

Jack kept reading the paper as I pondered her plain spoken words. Her directness was refreshing. I wondered if her succinct ways came out of a privileged upbringing, the fact she had been an only child, her artistic insights, or just what. It didn't matter to me because I liked this woman and her straight-shooting ways. In fact, earlier that day, Lucy Adele had told me, "One of the most important traits to develop is honesty. Honesty of feelings, dealings with other people . . . I think we'd avoid so many pitfalls if everyone was honest—honesty among nations, politicians, and family. I think simple honesty would make the world a better place."

"Lucy, what's wrong with the world? Everything seems to be so crazy and in a turmoil?" I asked. Lucy Adele looked up from her nimble fingers and needlework. She gave me one of her twinkle-feisty looks from across the den. The sides of her small mouth slightly lifted in a grin, and I knew something was coming.

"You tell me," she quipped with a chuckle. "I don't know the answers to these things." Without flinching, she said in a dry tone, "But let's decide all the answers in the next couple of days while you're here."

I broke out in laughter and the mood quickly changed. Jack mumbled something about getting another log on the fire and looking for his car keys. He was going to drive Lucy Adele and me through the Snake River Canyon to see the blooming orchards, white waterfalls, and fish hatcheries. Going for a drive through Magic Valley would be a nice outing.

"What ya looking for?" Lucy Adele asked Jack. She knew he was looking for his car keys. "Aren't you pretty sure they are in the car?" Jack walked out the back door and was out of hearing distance when Lucy Adele threw her head back and tried to restrain herself.

"You should hear us try to have a conversation," Lucy Adele snickered, referring to how forgetful both she and Jack, who was also seventy, had become.

"When we're trying to talk about someone, I'll say, 'Ol' what's his name . . . You know who I mean?' and Jack will say, 'Yeah, Ol' ah . . . I can't think of his name, but I know who you're talking about.' "

Lucy Adele got so tickled that tears slipped out of the corners of her eyes. She wiped them with a Kleenex. "And so," she struggled to finish between rushes of laughter, "Jack and I will have this whole conversation about someone and neither of us can remember the person's name."

We both doubled over with cackles. She caught her breath and then in stop-and-go phrases, she said,"The best thing . . . I did . . . recently . . . was . . . to wash my purse."

"You did what?" I yelped.

"I put it in the washing machine one evening when we left so it would be safe." She was laughing so hard by this time that she couldn't talk.

"The next morning I put a load of clothes in there and looked to see the water level," she choked, "And here was this . . . this big black thing floating around."

By this time, we were both hysterical and everything was funny. My sides were about to split. Just then Jack strolled through the back door with an armload of logs for the fire. He was holding his car keys. Lucy Adele took one look at the keys and roared again.

Jack looked at us with a manly smile, but he wasn't quite sure what was going on. He dropped a new log on the fire.

He drawled in his deep voice, "Before I can drive the car, I've got to take a short nap. I'd wreck us if I tried to drive, so we'll go later. Is that fair enough?" he asked, as he stood in front of the fireplace mantel and looked at Lucy Adele and me. Finally, we were both straight faced enough to answer.

"Sure."

"Sounds good to me," I said.

"We'll go in about an hour." Jack yawned as he walked past me and up the stairs to the bedroom.

Lucy Adele and I grinned at each other as she settled back down and returned to her exquisite needlepoint rug of butterflies and flowers. I wandered into the kitchen for a Coke and something to nibble on while Lucy Adele patiently made one stitch after another. How anyone could sit still that long was a wonder to me. How anyone could spend a year making one rug was even more of a wonder to me.

"I sure wouldn't want anyone walking on that rug if I were you," I hollered at Lucy Adele from the refrigerator.

"Barbara Bush walks on hers!" Lucy Adele called back, "and hers is much, much bigger than this one."

"Yeah, but she's the President's wife and she can show hers off," I teased.

Lucy Adele had completed several splendid needlepoint pieces over the years, everything from pictures to the upholstery on her father's favorite chair where he sat in the 1930s and listened to the radio, to making needlepoint Christmas stockings.

It was a total surprise when Lucy Adele made a mag-nificent needlepoint Christmas stocking in 1979 for my firstborn child, Rebekah, with glittery gold thread woven throughout her name and scenes of snowmen, carolers, and winter play across the bottom. It was lined with plush red velvet. The beauty of the stocking took my breath be-cause it was such a work of art. I knew it had taken Lucy Adele months to make it.

Then, without any prompting, she needlepointed two more Christmas stockings of equal artistry for my sons. She had stitched their names, Jed and Luke in bold col-ored thread across the top with reindeer, Ho-Ho-Ho, Santa, snow sledding, and other holiday scenes across the bottom and lined them in thick red velvet too. Lucy Adele didn't know it, but I told each of my children that these stockings were heirlooms and the long hours it took to make each one. I explained to Rebekah, Jed, and Luke that it was Lucy Adele's way of showing love for them. I told them all about the fair lady in Idaho.

"Sure glad all I had to needlepoint was 'Jed' instead of 'Jedidiah,' she said.

Carrying a Coke in my hand, I needed to stretch my legs before Jack woke up from his nap and before we left on our drive through the countryside. Being here was as comfortable as being in my own home back in Tennessee so I didn't feel it was impolite to stroll around the house. I knew Lucy Adele didn't care. Besides, I loved looking at all the furniture, glassware, oriental rugs, and other things that had belonged to Lucy Adele's mother and grand-mother. I especially liked the artwork hanging on the wallpapered walls. Most of it had been created by Lucy Adele or one of her five grown children, each of whom were very artistic in some way—either in painting, draw-ing, music, needlework, carpentry, or design. It was hard to believe there was so much talent in one family, but Lucy Adele's Idaho home where she and Jack had lived almost thirty-five years was bursting with it.

Over the fireplace in the den hung a large oil painting of a log cabin in the mountains, covered in deep snow, with a ten point buck standing in the center. It was a winter nighttime scene done in rich blue tones. This was one of several oils painted by Tom Ramsey, Lucy Adele's middle son, whose art was as good as any western artist's I had ever seen.

On the wall beside the bookcases were framed pen portraits of Jack and Lucy Adele drawn by Kirk Ramsey, their youngest son who was now thirty-five and who de- signed clothes and embroidery work for movie stars and entertainers like Angie Dickinson, Cher, Dolly Parton, Marie Osmond, and many others. Although Kirk had worked under the name of Rhett Turner in Los Angeles for several years, his dream was to develop his own line of clothes.

Guy Ramsey, the next to youngest son, was a photogra- pher and carpenter, and there were framed color photo- graphs of flowers and bees displayed near the breakfast table. He also had a talent with wood and had designed and built a striking bedroom suite for the log cabin where he lived. Not only did Guy have an artist's eye, but he had a craftsman's hands and could make anything out of wood.

Lucy Adele's only daughter, Camille, was a grant re- searcher for the Health and Science University in Port- land, Oregon, but she had a knack for beautiful needle- work like her mother. In fact, at one time, Camille owned and operated a craft and needlework shop along the coast of Oregon. Framed pieces of her handiwork hung on walls around Lucy Adele's house.

The oldest son, Jack, better known as "Jake" and in his mid-forties, was more like his father than any of the other grown children because he was the assistant manager of the West One Bank in the nearby town of Buhl. Yet, even Jake-the-banker had the ability to draw and was artistic. Lucy Adele shrugged her shoulders, "Nobody knows where these kids got all this talent!"

"You must be very proud," I said, admiring the many original oil paintings, watercolor paintings, needlepoint pieces and upholstery, as well as the lovely vases, glassware, Oriental rugs, and every other beautiful thing within my sight.

Lucy Adele raised her eyebrows and shook her head at me. Her usual crisp voice turned tender and low, "All this art work and possessions are not what's important."

Then she looked straight into my face with her pastel blue eyes and said, "A broken dish isn't as important as hurt feelings."

ཀ ཀ ཀ

We were only five minutes from the Filer elementary school where Lucy Adele had a 10:15 A.M. meeting, and we were hurrying out the back door when the telephone rang.

"Hello," Lucy Adele answered. "Yeah. You bet. I'll have Jack bring it right over." She hung up the telephone and rushed to the refrigerator and pulled out a congealed salad she had made to take to the Methodist church. There was a funeral this afternoon. She hollered at Jack and asked him to please take the salad to the church.

"Always something," she gasped as we rushed to the car.

"How did you get into helping kids learn how to read?" I asked as I drove the car down Yakima Street and turned left.

"A couple years ago, the first grade teacher asked if I knew anyone who would like to volunteer to help two little boys who were having a difficult time learning to read." She grinned, "The teacher knew full well that I would."

She pointed at the intersection for me to turn left again and there a few blocks away sat the rambling one-story grade school. The cheerful sounds of boys and girls running and yelling on the playground could be heard for blocks. It was recess.

"Yep, I've spent a lot of hours volunteering for things, but I've loved it all," Lucy Adele said, showing me where to park the car.

Just as we shut the car doors behind us, the school bell rang and children galloped in herds toward the double doors. Lucy Adele motioned for me to follow her down a wide corridor. The cement floors were carpeted to absorb noise and cut down on skinned knees and accidents. Along the concrete walls were bright drawings and water colored pictures done by the first and second graders. At the end of the building, we stopped in a lobby area in front of two third-grade classrooms. Dozens of nine-year-old boys and girls brushed by us on their way to their desks.

"Here's my Tavee!" Lucy Adele cheered. Instantly, she threw open her arms to a little freckle-faced, dark-haired boy with a bashful grin. He wore a black rumpled tee-shirt and stretch-pant black shorts and wornout sneakers. His brown hair was curly and uncombed, and his hands were scuffed and dirty from the playground. Lucy Adele pulled him close and gave him an affectionate squeeze. "Ah-h-h-h" she groaned with pleasure.

"How are ya? What's been goin' on? Have a good time at recess?" Lucy Adele shot questions at the brown-eyed boy. "I saw you in the program the other day, and I was proud of the way you guys sang. You did really well!"

Lucy Adele turned to me and with the pride of a grandmother. She introduced me to her reading student. "This is Tavee Christopher Klundt." The boy looked at me with shy, wide eyes and then back at his familiar friend, Mrs. Ramsey, who had been helping him learn to read for almost two years. Their smiles at each other showed deeper feelings than just as a teacher and student.

"We're gonna do some different things today, and I brought you something," Lucy Adele said as she pulled up the short chairs and table to begin the reading lessons. Tavee's eyes grew wider with expectation. The foyer was suddenly empty and quiet since all the other third graders were settled in their rooms and the doors were shut.

Lucy Adele pulled out a greeting card and handed it to Tavee to read. His eyes jumped, wondering what Mrs. Ramsey had brought him. She had given him a big card with a brown teddy bear on the front. Tavee opened the card and slowly read the words. Lucy Adele leaned in close to him, overlooking his efforts. There was a smile on her face that Tavee couldn't see.

Using his index finger to point at each word, Tavee slowly read, pausing after each word, "Bears—aren't—the—only—ones—who—need—hugs!" His voice was quiet and hesitant. He looked up at Mrs. Ramsey, then finished reading what she had written, "I—do—too,—Love, Mrs. Ramsey."

When Tavee looked up at his teacher, Mrs. Ramsey, he reached for her to give her a hug. Lucy Adele swelled with emotion.

"Yeah. Tavee's my real buddy," she murmured holding her feelings in check. She then handed him a toy glider. The pieces to the plane were made of lightweight balsa wood and were eight to ten inches long. She told him he would have to read the instructions in order to put it together. Three days a week, fifteen to twenty minutes each day, Lucy Adele would meet Tavee in the foyer at school and tutor him in reading. The first project they did was to read 150 pages. Sometimes they would go to the library and pick out a book together, but each lesson was structured to help Tavee recognize and pronounce words. When Tavee opened the glider plane, he looked across the foyer at me where I stood waiting next to the coat hooks along the wall.

With all the childlike freedom and openness that only a nine-year-old boy could have, Tavee exclaimed, "She's wonderful! She likes me cause she gives me hugs and reads to me."

At that moment, I thought Lucy Adele was going to burst. I felt like I would too. A rush of longing for my seven-year-old son, Jed, swept over me like a storm, and all I wanted to do was run and grab Tavee and hold him close. But, this wasn't my moment or my privilege. This love and friendship belonged to Lucy Adele, the seventy-year-old fair lady, and the cute and frumpy third-grade boy.

The twenty minutes with Tavee seemed like twenty seconds as Lucy Adele and I walked back to the car to drive home. Lucy Adele told me she did not think Tavee had a learning disability, but that his problem was a social one. She explained his vocabulary was neglected. He had little reference in his life to what written words meant because he sat in front of a televsion and rented movies too much of the time. His single mother worked, and no one had the time to read to him.

"I have a feeling I want to make somebody's life more meaningful and to make a difference. I don't have to make a difference to the world, but if I can make a difference to one person, then I've done something," Lucy Adele pondered. She looked over at me as I pulled into the driveway and stopped the car. I turned off the ignition.

"Wouldn't it be nice if Tavee could remember that at least I was there to love him? That's pretty important. And it's pretty important to have him love me too," she said softly.

I sat there a moment holding the steering wheel and thought about what Lucy Adele had said. As if time had stood still, the golden princess from so long ago was given another underprivileged friend to love.

Lucy Adele's Idaho Refrigerator Potatoes

Have you ever heard of refrigerator potatoes? It's a big recipe.

Take five pounds of potatoes, peel them, and cook them in boiling, salted water. Drain and mash until they are smooth. Then whip them good and blend in two three-ounce packages of cream cheese, a cup of sour cream, and two teaspoons of onion salt, one teaspoon salt, a quarter teaspoon pepper, and two tablespoons of butter. A little more butter always makes it good.

Blend all of it thoroughly, and after it cools completely, cover and put in the refrigerator. Then, you can dip into it and take out whatever you want for a meal or serving. They can be served with sprinkled cheese, chives, green onions, or whatever.

I got this recipe from my hairdresser. Young mothers these days don't have time to start with real potatoes, so they use instant. This is a convenient way to have delicious, real potatoes. If you're going to have a party, heat them at a low temperature, 300 degrees for thirty-five minutes. It makes a beautiful casserole for company.

They're more elegant than mashed potatoes.

❧ ❧ ❧

Chapter Seven

HELP FROM THE BAYOU

SHARON WAS EXCITED. She had never been to the bayou country of the deep South and had always wanted to go. She had read and heard about "bayous" but like most people, they were strange places written about in geography books, such as the Amazon River or rain forests in South America. They were places where movies were made and which environmentalists tried to save, but now, she would see for herself the mysterious wetlands near the Gulf of Mexico.

"I asked the other teachers at school to tell me what a bayou was and none of them knew," she laughed. Sharon Cook was a single woman, thiry-six years old, and had worked as a kindergarten teacher since she graduated from Middle Tennessee State University. She stood about 5' 4", was trim and stylish, and wore her long brown hair accented with blonde highlights. She reminded me of the famous actress and singer, Ann Margaret. Sharon's face was pretty with big brown-black eyes, and she looked especially attractive in bright colors against her olive skin. Although she had skied in Colorado, attended theaters in New York, worked out at a health club, spent vacations in Acapulco, toured the Grand Canyon, and had a wide range of cultural and travel experiences, she had never been to bayou country.

"How would you like to join me to visit an old friend of mine?" I asked Sharon one day. "My friend lives right on a bayou near the Gulf." Like me, Sharon had an adventurous streak and jumped at the chance.

Over the past couple of years, Sharon and I had become friends after meeting in a Sunday school class at church. On the weekends when she did not have a date and my three children were visiting with their father and stepmother, Sharon and I would go to the movies, try new and quaint restaurants, visit museums or libraries, play tennis, and more. She was fun, and I was glad she could join me.

The long drive south from Nashville took over nine hours, and we were well stocked with cookies, Cokes, and pretzels. Slowly, as the miles and hours passed, the landscape began to change from Tennessee's rolling hills of hardwood trees and valleys with rockbottomed streams, to wet lowlands. As far as the eye could see, there was pancake flatness and spindly pine trees reaching high into the sky reminding me of toothpicks. The ground had changed from dark dirt where farmers plowed, to red clay, then to marshes and swamps. Some of the loblolly pines were gnarled and twisted, bent from the last hurricane that had whipped them back and forth. Most of the deep South knew the wrath of fickle hurricanes stretching one hundred miles across and generating winds at or above two hundred miles per hour. Some of them, like Camille in 1969 and Frederick in 1979, would rise up out of the sea like violent monsters and devour everything in their path—blowing away houses, businesses, cars, livestock, and people. What wasn't blown apart was drowned in the torrential rains and giant wave walls that would flood coastal towns.

Each mile brought Sharon and me closer to bayou country. The Choctaw Indians had named them "bayuk." That was their word for creek—small waterways, weaving and turning in every direction like twisted vines, mysterious and closed in by jungle-like swamps. There were no more mountains, no rolling hills, no rock cliffs . . . only silent shadows, sleeping waters of dark liquid, and cypress trees draped in Spanish moss. This moss hung from trees and swayed like grey ghosts in gentle Gulf breezes.

We were in the land of romance and dreams, a place where earth couldn't decide if it was land or water. Like love, there was always the mystery and the struggle between the two. My longtime friend, Jan Taggart and her husband, Bob, lived here, at the end of a narrow lane with a winding bayou wrapped around their yard. It had been over a year since I had seen Jan, but we talked by phone almost every week and had been close friends for nearly twenty years.

"Wow!" Sharon exclaimed. "This is incredible," she said, pointing to a watery marsh full of pines, cypress trees, waxy magnolias, dense underbrush, willows, and grasses. A great blue heron stood motionless at the edge of the marsh. Then another heron glided down from an overcast sky and perched next to the first one.

Sharon needed this brief change from her kindergarten classroom of energetic five year olds. The serenity of this place was a sharp contrast to what she had been going through in her personal life for the past several months. Sharon's mother had been diagnosed with terminal cancer and her days were numbered. She might live two weeks, two months, or die tomorrow. Although her mother was not in pain and still able to function around the house, Sharon had stayed close at hand, available at a moment's notice. Our trip to the quiet bayou was what Sharon needed, a rest from the strain, and time to reflect; but if that certain telephone call came, Sharon would fly home to Tennessee. Sharon told me her family had picked out the casket for her mother and had made the necessary funeral arrangements last week. She described the casket, the color and lining, how much it cost, the burial plot, pallbearers, on and on. As she told me these things, I felt helpless and uneasy. I didn't know what to say, or how to respond. It was easier for me to talk about the latest movie, her students, a new book, my children, or anything besides death or dying. I wanted to pretend this wasn't happening. Although I thought of myself as a caring friend, I wasn't the best person to talk to when it came to these matters. I avoided those subjects like the plague and preferred having fun and good times.

As we turned down the narrow lane headed toward Jan's house, I was thinking about Jan's happy smile, Bob's easy ways, a tasty supper, and a weekend of laughs. Jan was loads of fun and loved antiques. I knew she'd have some old piece of furniture or relic to show me. We might go antiquing or shopping or stay up all night giggling like college girls. *That's just what Sharon needed,* I thought to myself. *Get her mind on something else . . .*

Being here was like stopping at the end of the world and getting off the merry-go-round, away from morbid thoughts, and the last place you'd expect anything out of the ordinary to happen. Little did Sharon or I know what was ahead. We were both in for a weekend that would change us forever.

ﺩﺍ ﺩﺍ ﺩﺍ

It was almost dark, a soft dusk, but I could see Jan waiting behind the front door of her hundred-year-old home, sheltered under tall pines and surrounded by live oaks, magnolias, and thick swamps. I blew my horn and stopped in the shell driveway. Just as I expected, her smile was there and the twinkle in her eyes. She ran out to meet us, across the wooden porch, laughing all the way. Sharon and Jan embraced each other upon introduction, and both seemed glad to meet and make a new friend. I knew they would. Arm in arm, Jan and I walked past the rose beds up the walkway, jabbering so fast neither of us could finish a sentence before the other interrupted.

Even though Jan was somewhat older than I, we had been friends for a long time. We first met back in 1972, working in a government school program where she was the registered nurse, and I was the freshly graduated social worker. From the beginning, we were like two sparks, always charging the other, and between the two of us, we thought there was no problem or person we couldn't fix. She was one of the most exciting and spontaneous women I had ever known, full of life and energy. So much so, she only required two to four hours sleep per night and often got up and read, watched television, studied, or spent time in thought while her husband slept. Although she would soon be fifty-five years old, Jan looked and acted much younger. There was a spring in her step and an enthusiasm about every part of her life, from being a nurse, a wife, mother, grandmother, homemaker, to her love of antiques. She was girlish. She told me she thought successful women were really little girls.

"Women who forget that little girl part of themselves are clamoring for power to the point where they get lost along the way, and the joy goes out of what they're trying to do," she said. "I hope none of us ever grow up. If we lose that child, we lose the essence of life."

She kept her weight around 125 pounds, always careful to control it because she wasn't very tall, only 5′ 3″. She wore her thick gray hair short and swept up on the sides and curly on top. Her lips were full and they complemented her oval face and dark complexion. But it was always her eyes that were distinct. I had never seen eyes like them before. They weren't big, deep, sultry, or glamourous, and it was hard to determine their color. Sometimes they were grey, or green, or blue, depending on what colors she wore, but more so, they were translucent, like liquid diamonds that glittered. They were unclouded and seemed open all the way inside. Whatever it was about her eyes, they were alive, sometimes floating, sometimes aflame.

Jan had spent over twenty years as a registered nurse and professional health care educator, working in hospitals, health care agencies, and teaching seminars and workshops from New York to Texas. She had started nursing school in Seattle, Washington, then transferred to another school in Los Angeles, California, near her home town of Redondo Beach and attended there until she became engaged to Bob and married him in 1956.

"When I was nine years old, I knew being a nurse was what I wanted to be," she said. "My aunt was a registered nurse and at that time, nurses wore starched, white uniforms with long sleeves, a navy blue cape with red lining, and a cap. I can see it as if it were yesterday—my aunt going off to work in her blue cape and my heart would just go pitty-pat," Jan chuckled and thumped her chest. "I would say, I'm gonna do that when I grow up and have one of those capes," she laughed. "I never had one because by the time I grew up, capes were a thing of the past."

After she and Bob married, they lived in California for seven years where their sons, Andy, Jon, and Jim, were born. Bob was working for a large oil company there but was being transferred to help start up a new refinery in the deep South. With three children, the youngest only thirteen months old, Bob had waited to tell Jan about the transfer until one day when he handed her a Chamber of Commerce booklet promoting the South.

"How would you like to be a Southern Belle?" he asked.

"A what?" she said. "How soon do I have to let you know?"

"Tomorrow."

Their house went up for sale and it sold in two days. The next thing Jan knew, she was transplanted from popular California beaches, cool dry air, busy cities with museums, theaters, shopping and activities to a tiny Southern town where there was 90 percent humidity, mosquitoes, marshes, swamps, and hurricanes. "Coming from California, it was culture shock," she mused, "but, I was ready for a change, and it seemed right to me. I had lived all my life at a running pace. I talked and walked fast, still do, and did everything in a hurry, but down here in the South, it's very laid back, and people just don't get into a hurry." She paused and thought a moment. "At least I stop and smell the roses."

For the last couple of years, Jan had made the decision to slow down even more. After working as a nurse and health educator for years and years, often eighty hours a week, carrying a beeper, being on call twenty-four hours a day and passing Bob in their driveway as she rushed to catch another plane to lead a seminar, she decided it was time to stop. Since their three sons were grown, married, and had families of their own, Jan believed she and Bob needed to spend more time together besides two tired days on the weekends.

"One day I looked at my husband across the table. He had been traveling, gone and only home on the weekend, and I'm working sixteen hours a day. He came home, and I'm *still* working. I looked at him and said, 'What are we doing? Where are we going with all this?' " There was tension in her voice as she remembered those days. Then with quiet resolution she added, "Because I have given to everyone else, now it's time for me to give to my family. That's where I am." She raised her eyebrows and those eyes of hers glistened. She leaned forward, "I haven't lost those professional skills. I can still help people."

ﾏ ﾏ ﾏ

Bob Taggart was waiting on us in the old fashioned den. When Jan ushered us in, he stood tall like a 6' 3" sculpture, lean and proud. In his late fifties, he looked distinguished wearing a dark suit, and his gray hair and sharp blue eyes made him very handsome. Bob had just returned home to the bayou from a business trip in Chicago where it was freezing and blowing snow. Down here it was seventy degrees and balmy. Bob was an easy man to like because he was thoughtful, a hard worker, and very kind. Through the years, I had grown to admire and respect him because of his honesty, dedication to his family, and expertise in the oil industry. He was a smart man and not much of a talker, but when he spoke, I listened because his words carried meaning.

After hugs and introductions and unloading the car, Sharon and I got settled in the guest bedroom. The big iron bed was white and covered with a handmade quilt for a spread. Ruffled drapes blended with the soft colored wallpaper, and old tables, books, and momentos were displayed around the room. Hanging on the wall over an oak chest of drawers was one of Jan's crossstitch pieces. It read, "We're glad to have you as our guest, hope you have a good night's rest, tomorrow you again may roam, but while you're here, just feel at home." It was stitched in burgundy with a pineapple at the bottom. The pineapple was a symbol of hospitality.

Everywhere we looked, in every room, there were relics and keepsakes—antique tables, photographs, quilts, crafts, wall hangings, and handmade treasures. Jan began to show us around. She pointed out a cobalt blue dresser set she had found in Arkansas. It was a set of delicate dishes where ladies from long ago stored their combs, brushes, lost hair, and hairpins. Fancy little hankies decorated the edge of old pictures. A vintage nursing gown was displayed on one wall while a seventy-five-year-old pair of lace-up boots hung on another.

"I just love your home," Sharon cooed. "It's so unique and unusual."

Jan slapped her hands and thought of something else. She clicked her heels across the wooden floors and asked us to follow her back into the den. She walked in a hurry. Bob had changed into his comfortable coveralls and was resting and reading the newspaper in a reclining chair. Behind him, hanging on the wall over his lamp table was another one of Jan's framed hand-stitched pieces. She loved to cross-stitch and was very skilled at needlework. It read, "Southerner . . . A Person Born or Living in the South, Gracious, Easy Going, Slow Talking, Friendly Folk Devoted to Front Porches, Oak Trees, Cool Breezes, Magnolias, Peaches, and Fried Chicken." That verse seemed perfect next to Bob.

"This is known as a Hoosier," Jan beamed. "I've been wanting one for ten years." It was a tall baking cabinet used in kitchens fifty to one hundred years ago. There were cupboards on the top and bottom with a flat counter in the middle to roll-out biscuits and prepare meals. Old spice jars sat on racks inside the cupboard doors. Across from the Hoosier sat an antique oak icebox. A hand-hewn kitchen table was in the center of the den and kitchen. Here, Jan and Bob sat in the mornings to eat breakfast, drink their coffee, and watch the bayou and birds out the back window.

For the next half hour, we ooo-ed, and aaahhh-ed over Jan's collections. There were butter and ice cream churns, old tool chests, crocks, shipping crates, dolls, and more. Sharon and I felt as if we had gone backward in time to an era of simplicity. Jan showed us her favorite piece of furniture, a mahogany secretary with beveled glass and mirrors. She kept it in her dining room.

"Most of this stuff wouldn't mean a thing to anybody, but it does to us," she said.

ᴥ ᴥ ᴥ

Jan prepared a late evening dinner of hot broccoli soup and chicken salad sandwiches on flaky croissants. Her iced tea was smooth and southern. We ate on a gracious table in the dining room with century old plates that were so thin and light, they were transparent. I felt clumsy, and hoped I wouldn't chip or crack something whenever my fork hit the plate. The tea goblets were also ancient, and I wondered if they were strong enough to hold the ice cubes. We had fresh peaches for dessert and drank aromatic coffee out of delicate cups that matched the plates. Our dinner was in keeping with the historic furniture, laced tablecloth, fragile dishes, and slow moving bayou that surrounded us all.

Sharon was eager to please and helped Jan clear the table after everyone finished their last bite of peaches. I enjoyed watching Sharon and Jan become better acquainted and appreciated what was happening. They were conversing like they had known each other for years, both friendly and asking questions about the other as they walked back and forth from the kitchen to the dining room. Sharon loaded the dishwasher with pans and bowls while Jan handwashed the easily broken dishes. They were laughing. I took a deep breath and was glad to see Sharon having a good time and taking a break from her troubles. This would be a time for her to forget about Tennessee and her mother's terminal cancer and focus on happier things. As they chatted back and forth, I decided to catch up on Bob and find out what was happening in the oil business.

"Yeah," Bob drawled. "We produce 300,000 barrels a day and are working on heavy oils." He began to talk about the refinery where he worked as an operating supervisor for the past thirty-five years. "We got over a thousand men working and are fully automated. The plant goes twenty-four hours a day, 365 days a year," he said. "The only thing that's ever brought the refinery down is a hurricane.

He explained how they moved all the working men out of the plant but would keep a skeleton crew during a hurricane. Bob had been in charge of the skeleton crew during several hurricanes, and it was his job to keep the refinery from being blown away.

"We just hired twenty-four operators but interviewed 3,000 people for those twenty-four jobs. We're a great company, always here, and it's a shame we couldn't hire a lot of them." Bob was sipping fresh coffee out of his choice mug that had a picture of a dairy cow and barnyard on it. Since Bob had been raised on a farm, the cup probably reminded him of his childhood. Whenever he set the cup down, I could read words across the top. "Some days you step in it and some days you don't."

I was fascinated with Bob's work at the refinery and wished I could understand more about the chemical process of changing oil into jet fuel, gasoline, asphalt, and other products. As he tried to make the complicated process easy for me to grasp, talking in his slow style, I could hear bits and pieces of Sharon's conversation with Jan as they stood facing each other by the kitchen sink. The kitchen, dining room, and den were open so I could see them out of the corner of my eye. Jan's hands were waving in the air. She leaned closer to Sharon and her voice raised in pitch. Whatever they were talking about was getting louder and so was my curiosity. I had one ear open to Bob and the oil business, and the other ear directed toward the kitchen.

"Nothing is guaranteed where people and relationships are concerned," Jan cried. "Every relationship is a risk!" Her voice was forceful. "Sometimes it's not until we're backed into a corner that we finally recognize what direction we need to go," she added.

Sharon stood motionless, staring into Jan's clear eyes. I suspected they were talking about men and marriage and how afraid Sharon was to get married. Sharon had been engaged to marry before. She had gone through some disappointing relationships and was at another place of decision in her personal love life. In the short time since we arrived, Sharon had learned how easy it was to talk with Jan. She sensed Jan was a caring person, open, and a good listener. Although there were others who would listen, Sharon liked Jan's bullseye truthfulness and honest answers to her questions.

In her mid-thirties, Sharon had watched many child-hood friends go through divorce, had seen religious leaders and politicians run around on their wives, and had witnessed many broken hearts. In her mind, there were too many ill-intentioned men in the world. So, she didn't know who or what to believe. All the things she had heard in Sunday school about marriage didn't seem to work in this day and age. At least not with the people she knew—certainly not with the rich and famous either. Sharon was discouraged and skeptical about who to trust, finding true love, and how to know who is right for you. She fired one question after another at Jan.

"Is trust earned, or something that's there from the beginning?" Sharon asked. She stacked the antique dishes carefully on the counter as she dried them.

"Trust is something that grows," Jan answered. "I do think it is earned. I can't say I'm going to trust you with everything I've got since I just met you, but as you get to know someone, you grow to trust them . . . because . . . they . . . prove . . . themselves . . . trustworthy!" Jan drew her words out to make sure Sharon understood.

Sharon looked strained and downcast. "I don't know anyone my age who is happily married, and I'm trying to see what makes a marriage work." She sighed. "Being alike or being different or what?" Although Jan was not aware of what was going on in Sharon's personal love life, she probably sensed the reasons for the questions. Jan's diamond eyes cut to the center and weren't easily fooled.

Jan was quick to respond. "Both have to decide if it's important enough to make it work. And, I think it's a solid love and commitment to each other, so much so that nothing can break it apart." She paused to think a moment about what had kept her thirty-four-year marriage together. "In any relationship, there will be times you dis-

agree, but marriage is a partnership. Just because you become a couple doesn't mean you lose your identity. Don't
allow yourself to become an extension of another person.
You are an individual in your own right. Bob and I allow
each other to be individuals." Without any apology or ex-
planation, Jan added, "We give each other space!"

Sharon dried another dish, deep in thought. She
seemed confused. What Jan was saying sounded good, but
she'd heard that kind of general advice before. Everyone,
especially church goers, talked about love and commitment. However, Sharon knew married people, even
churchgoers, who were committed to the institution of
marriage but didn't really love each other and were more
like college roommates, or strangers living under the same
roof for convenience sake, financial security, or out of fear
of being alone. They stayed married out of commitment
and not out of love. On the other hand, she knew couples
who said they loved each other, yet weren't committed to
marriage.

Then, among her professional friends, she had seen
married couples give each other space only to grow apart.
She had seen successful women have their own individual
identities and find their husband had left them for another woman. What was it that made some marriages
work and others fail? What was missing? What was the
illusive ingredient?

"To this very day, I would live in a tent with Bob. He
is predictable, and I'm spontaneous, but the bottom line is
that our value system is the same. We have the same goals
and want the same things in life," Jan said.

"But what about chemistry?" Sharon was puzzled. "Isn't
there supposed to be some of that?"

"Our problem as women is that we've been taught
there's supposed to be this zip-zap and fireworks," Jan said

shaking her head. Her voice was getting excited and carried all over the house. "Lasting relationships come from being able to be comfortable with each other—be just who you are," she said emphatically. She paced the floor, in her California hurry, trying to stay cool and philosophical.

Jan was moving across the kitchen floor with her arms outstretched and the palms of her hands wide open. She talked not only with her voice, but with her hands, her eyes, and her entire body. Whatever she said, she seemed to throw her entire self into communicating with another person. She leaned close to Sharon. "There was never an electric chemistry between Bob and me. No fireworks, my heart didn't thump. A wall doesn't have to fall on everybody," Jan said. "In the first place, I've discovered through the years working with people that, usually, those particular relationships don't last."

I knew Sharon was getting an ear full and probably hearing things she hadn't heard or read before. The romance novels and fashion magazines that flooded grocery stores, number one songs on the radio, and award winning sexy movies did not present love as being something "comfortable." Comfortable? Come on.

Recently, Sharon and I had made wisecracks about some of the alluring headlines on magazines in the grocery store: "When Happily Marrieds are Secretly Unfaithful," and "I've Got a Better Body Than I Had At Twenty," and "Has Your Love Life Cooled Off?" and "Yes! You Can Have A Better Butt." We noticed how every woman's magazine on the racks had articles about your body, or sex, or shaky marriages. According to the world, love was passion, excitement, magic, dynamite, and bigger than life. Everyone deserved it. And, like millions of other singles, why wouldn't Sharon want a charismatic person who would sweep her mind and body away?

But Jan had a way of challenging mainstream ideas. This was one of the many attributes I admired about Jan. She had backed me against the wall many times over the years and had confronted me on issues from religion to money to evolution. Although she was a lively person, Jan was a thinker and a motivator and resisted people who settled for one-of-the-crowd answers to life. Not only did Jan have an open heart, she had an open and intelligent mind. She thought, questioned, analyzed, reasoned, and refused to believe or accept every trend that came along— especially trends about love and marriage.

"What about sex?" Sharon asked, trying to throw Jan off guard. Sharon was smart, too, and not afraid to pin Jan down. She knew Jan was from an older generation and talking about sex was probably off limits and too private. Women who were Jan's age were more reserved and often prudish when it came to sex. Many women Jan's age thought sex was a duty or dirty. Maybe Jan would be embarrassed. I could hear the dare in Sharon's voice.

Jan spinned around like a dancer and without blinking an eye, she said, "My concept on sex is that it's *great!*" Sharon giggled and was stopped in her tracks. She had not expected to hear Jan say that. She was liking Jan more by the minute.

"I also believe you have to put sex into perspective. How much time do you spend in bed?" Jan asked shrugging her shoulders. "Take that versus how much time you spend out of bed? There's too much everyday stuff that takes place more often than the bedroom scene, and the bedroom scene ain't gonna work if the rest of it isn't working." Sharon nodded in agreement as if to urge Jan to tell more. Sharon couldn't believe this woman she just met was able to zero in on such intimate problems. *Didn't everyone have sexual problems?* Sharon wondered. If not, why were videos, movies, articles, books, and magazines instructing the public how to have good sex, more sex, safe sex, and how to keep your partner, or several partners, panting for more? It was becoming harder and harder to sort through what was true and what wasn't.

Jan popped the drain in the sink and rested herself against the counter. "You have to be a friend of the person, enjoy being with that person. Bob and I cultivated a friendship and fell in love long before anything physical started happening." Sharon began to interrupt but Jan came on like a brewing storm. It angered Jan to see young women like Sharon misled by half-truths and Hollywood notions. There were as many lies about love and sex as there were tabloids on sale at the check-out counters in grocery stores.

"You think that when you're not turned on everytime you look at this hunk, then something must be wrong?" Jan asked. Her eyes were becoming brighter and looked like radar. "That you can't possibly love him?" Once more, she faced Sharon eye to eye.

Jan's face was flushed with fire. "That's garbage!" she cried. She was angry, and there was fury in her movements as she wiped out the sink. "I gradually came into the knowledge I was falling into love with Bob. Never did it zap me. Even after marriage, I learned to love him more and more and more." Just as though Jan and Sharon were standing in the eye of a storm, everything became still and quiet. Dead seconds passed. Then, without warning and with the force of a hurricane wind, it came. There was no time to prepare for the moment.

Jan threw her arms in the air, and with her whole being, there came an earnest, heartfelt cry, "*Love is not a result of sex!*"

Her words crashed through Sharon's questions and media-soaked mind. They were like gales blowing trash out of a room and leaving it clean. With another gust, Jan finished what she had started, "*Satisfying sex is a result of love!*"

❧ ❧ ❧

"The elevation out here in the yard in low spots is only three feet above sea level," Bob mumbled at a pace that made a turtle seem fast. His voice never changed from an even hum. He was explaining why there was water in the yard from the bayou and how one of their dogs, ol' Jake, got eaten by an alligator. I wondered if Bob heard any of the commotion in the other room. If he did, he was happy to leave it alone. This was an example of what Jan meant when she said, "We give each other space."

In reality, Bob was content to allow Jan to be herself and to answer Sharon's questions however she wished. Jan could stand on her head, skip around the room, or sing from the front porch, and that would be all right. Bob had no desire or need to control or manipulate her behavior.

"I don't think a man should dominate his wife because it makes it harder on the man. Let her handle herself, and that takes the burden off him," he said.

His attitude about marriage was simple, "Find a man who likes to dig in the dirt, and be careful that financial success is not his top goal because that's not meaningful." Bob's few words were like servings of rich food to eat in small bites and chew on for a long time. There was profound truth and nutrition in what he said.

❧ ❧ ❧

What happened the next day in the television room was unplanned and life-changing. It had nothing to do with men, sex, or marriage and was one of those experiences in life that comes as a surprise. Like natural wonders such as Niagara Falls, the Grand Canyon or the Great Pyramids, Sharon and I were astonished and amazed.

Bob was outside talking to his rose garden and digging in the dirt while we girls played and did what females do. Giggle. Talk. Giggle. We had fresh Cokes, pretzels, and bread sticks to munch on while we lounged in front of the television. I was feeling like the true vacationer as I sipped on my cold Coke and made wisecracks. This was the life. Easy does it, down on the bayou. Sharon also seemed relaxed and far away from her concerns. I was glad to see her laughing and having a good time.

We heard the screech of a hoot owl in the swamp and then the blast of a shotgun. I jumped and was startled. Jan explained some boys further down the bank had been shooting, but she didn't know at what. It was illegal to shoot alligators although they were becoming overpopulated and a threat to dogs and cats and young children. Jan was perturbed about one alligator who visited her yard most of the summer. The ten-foot gator would slink up out of the bayou and settle down to sunbathe in her secluded yard while she tried to sunbathe by the swimming pool.

"Did you offer him some sun-screen lotion?" I teased.

"I'll tell you what . . . I about offered him some buck-shot!" Jan countered. She propped her feet upon the large wooden crate that sat in front of the plaid sofa. The square crate was like a coffee table. "It's so wonderful to get out of shoes!" Jan sighed. "I cannot stand to wear shoes." After I made a few comments about smelly feet, I propped my barefeet on the crate too. All we needed was popcorn to feel like we were in the movies as we loafed in front of the color TV. We weren't really watching anything, but had the television turned low in the background. Yes sir, I was a long way from feeding, dressing, and driving three kids to and from school, doing four loads of laundry each morning, cleaning the house and scrubbing toilets and tubs, paying bills, boiling hotdogs and burning toast, helping with homework, being the taxi to piano lessons and museums, then squeezing six hours of writing and office business in between, and falling into bed every night, an exhausted single working parent. I could understand why that ol' alligator liked to lay back and take it easy around here. This was one of those times when everything seemed ridiculous and funny. I felt free and goofy and silly and was waiting for Jan to say or do something so I could poke fun. I was eager for some belly laughs and wanted to kick-up my heels, roll on the floor, and hang loose with every joke I could remember. I even giggled to myself, thinking about Jan and that ugly alligator sunbathing together, like Ozzie and Harriet, or Mutt and Jeff. Instead of the old grade school book about Dick and Jane that read, "See Jane run," it was more like "See JAN run" . . . On and on my mind played. What a cute couple they must have been beside the swimming pool and bayou. The beauty and the beast. I was chuckling under my breath when Sharon quietly spoke up.

"My mother is dying right now."

Like sticking a needle in a hot air balloon, all the humor in my mind and laughs in my throat went p-o-o-f. Evaporated. Gone. Sharon's comment was as heavy as a truckload of bricks and brought me headlong into another state of mind. I didn't know what to say or do. Obviously, Sharon was not able to leave her worries behind.

As if she were in a hospital emergency room, Jan automatically clicked back into being the professional nurse. Jan was not pacing the floor, giggling, or excitable like she had been the day we arrived. Instead, she was sober and in control. Jan did not act alarmed or uneasy because she was equipped and well-trained how to react in a crisis situation. To me, this was a crisis. Unlike me, Jan was not afraid to talk to Sharon about her mother's illness. There was much for me to learn from this encounter, and I would be better off to keep quiet and listen. Like other adventures I had experienced, this was new territory, and I needed to keep my eyes and ears open. I sensed something meaningful was in the works. I could feel it because of the solemn mood that fell on the room and the color television grew dim in comparision. I sipped my Coke and swallowed nervously.

Collected and cool, Jan flipped off the television with a remote control panel. "How long has she been diagnosed? Has she been in pain?"

Sharon began to talk, hesitantly at first. She told Jan her mother had been diagnosed with lung cancer about a year ago and was in the last stages of the disease. Her mother was not taking cancer treatments because there was no hope. Fortunately, her mother was not in any pain but was rapidly losing her ability to think clearly and remember what she had eaten for breakfast an hour before. The past year had been a long ordeal and trial for Sharon and her family, and they all hoped it would be quick.

"We've made most of the arrangements," Sharon said. Her chest heaved with a long sigh. Her voice was flat and without emotion. "I just don't want her to suffer."

"People die different ways," Jan said softly.

"What if I'm not there, and she dies? What do you say to me then? There's so much I want to do for my mother. How can I talk to her now? How do I get her to open up?" Sharon's dry and direct questions tumbled out like a broken concrete dam. She had been pent up and was bursting with suppressed doubts and unresolved questions. She was determined to be strong and brave and tried to conceal what she was feeling. With the tenderness of feeding a newborn lamb, Jan began to answer Sharon's questions. I could see warmth float out of Jan's eyes toward Sharon as if to assure Sharon that she truly understood.

Sharon did not know everything about Jan's professional background. For the last eight years of her career as a nurse, Jan had led seminars on death and dying. She had been a counselor to terminally ill patients and their families all across America. The administrator at the hospital where Jan worked thought Jan's counseling program was innovative and a valuable service. She was given an executive-type office in the hospital. It wasn't long until over a hundred doctors were referring patients to Jan for counseling and her program mushroomed. Jan became a team member with the doctors and clergymen, helping families make it through their loss. Sometimes, she worked with families for years after the death of the patient. Her counseling program began to fill a big hole in serving the hospital and the bereaved families. Doctors liked what she was doing because it took precious time and pressure off them. Word of her success traveled to the state university, and Jan was commissioned by the medical facility of the university to write a whole semester's curriculum on death and dying. After she completed the curriculum, she presented her program to twelve Ph.D's from Louisiana, Alabama, and Mississippi.

Jan looked at Sharon through the tried-and-tested eyes of experience and with great care. "If anybody needs somebody who's gonna listen to them, it's somebody who's dying," Jan explained. "You talk to a dying person just like anyone else. They are a person. A person who happens to be dying." There was stillness in the room as Sharon and I sat watching every move Jan made. We were captivated by her wisdom and know-how. She was the teacher and we were the students. We waited patiently for whatever she wanted to tell us.

"Nobody wants to be around someone who has cancer or is dying cause they don't know what to say or how to act. Death is a threat and reminds us of our own mortality. Actually, I didn't 'counsel' my patients; I just listened. Most of the time I let them do the talking or if they didn't want to talk, I'd just sit there with them for awhile." Jan cleared her throat. The silence that surrounded us was penetrating. Just then, the grandfather clock in the old-fashioned den chimed softly, sounding like a church bell off in the distance. "Today, people are isolated in hospital rooms where back fifty years ago, people died at home with the whole family unit involved and supporting each other. A person who is dying is the last person who should be alone."

Jan's tone of voice was soothing and in harmony with the bells from the grandfather clock, reminding me where we were. Sharon's brown eyes got bigger as she kept them glued on Jan's face. I could see the wheels turning in Sharon's brain.

As if Jan could read Sharon's mind, she quickly said, "Those of us standing by have to give the dying person permission to die anyway they want. And—when—they want. It's their right. Whether you are there or not will not make any difference because that person will die anyway. You know, I've seen people wait to die until a certain family member—husband, wife, or child—left the room," Jan told us. Sharon was perplexed. *Could people near death choose the moment to die? Why would a dying person wait until someone left the room?* Sharon wondered about it all. "Maybe the person dying wanted to spare that family member," Jan said, thoughtfully.

"But, what can I *do?*" Sharon pleaded.

"The exciting thing is, all we have to do is 'just be.'" That's the only way we can truly love or truly help," Jan answered quietly.

"Just be?" Sharon cried. "What do you mean?"

Jan was very matter of fact. "Stop trying! Relax. Quit struggling and *just be.*" Jan ended her comments as abruptly as if she had run into the Great Wall of China. Jan purposely stopped talking because she wanted to allow those two words, *just be*, to hang in the air and fall gently on Sharon's troubled soul. After what seemed like a long time, Jan smiled at Sharon and finished. "All we have to do is *be* an instrument of love, not constantly using our own energies or striving to *do* something."

This advice was foreign to Sharon who was a high achiever. Sharon's whole life had been built on working hard, performing well in college and graduate school, being busy in church, doing charity work, and improving her status in society. Sharon was used to earning her way, earning the love and favor of others by *doing* good works. And now that her mother was dying, there must be something more she could *do*. How could she just be? Sharon thought this concept *just be* sounded shallow. *Be what?*

"Where do you get this idea?" Sharon challenged. "I've never heard or read this before. Why do you want to listen to dying people, anyway? Isn't it depressing? Besides, aren't you afraid to die?" Sharon's dark eyes jumped with confrontations. I liked being the spectator, sitting in the comfortable easy chair with my bare feet propped on the big crate, and watching the two of them meet head on. Sharon aimed for the intellect while Jan shot for the heart. Sparks zoomed back and forth between them.

The ball was in Jan's court, and I could see her bracing herself to come out with full force. Sharon didn't know what she had done. There was a hot button in Jan's private life, and Sharon had just punched it. Jan half grinned like an ol' pro ready to make a decisive move. Jan was very careful how she advanced. Instinctively, I sat up straight and waited for what was next.

"I don't worry whether people believe my story because I know I experienced it," Jan said confidently. "People have their own choice as to whether they believe it or not."

With that, Sharon's curiosity was aroused and her attitude cautious but receptive. She leaned forward in her chair, placing her elbows on her knees with her hands under her chin as if to say, "come on, let's hear it."

Jan began her story. It happened back in April, 1971, while Jan was working on a shift in the surgical unit at the hospital. Because certain antibiotics had to be given by a registered nurse, Jan was asked to give all medicines to the patients while the other registered nurse on duty made rounds.

There was a certain antibiotic drug called Keflin™ the doctors used frequently after surgery to prevent patients from getting an infection. It helped give the patients an edge. Jan had been giving Keflin™ and all other medicines to patients everyday for over two months while she had been working in the surgical unit. Some patients would get two or three doses of it a day, every six hours, and there were several patients taking it. The drug came in a powder form, and Jan had to mix it with sterile water.

"It made me itch, react a little bit. If anyone had ever told me that I could have a reaction to this antibiotic, or any medication, just by administering it to someone else, I would have told them they were crazy," Jan cried. "I didn't take the medicine. I gave it!"

She gave the last two doses of medicine and by the time she returned to the nurses' station, her eyes were itching. Then she started itching around her mouth. She began to scratch her face and swallowed an allergy pill to counteract the itching. Twenty minutes passed. Jan had turned in her medical reports, and it was close to 3:30 P.M.—quitting time. She planned to go home when all of a sudden, she felt like she was on fire.

"I felt like somebody had taken two torches and put them on my eyes. My chest began to hurt, and I knew I was having bronchial spasms." She decided to go down to the emergency room to get examined, hoping the doctor on duty could give her something to make her feel better. "I walked down the stairs, didn't even take an elevator," Jan chuckled.

She was lying on one of the treatment tables chatting with the emergency room doctor, making small talk about the weather and time to go home. Then she started to feel nauseated and sick so she told the doctor she felt very ill. He walked over to the table and after he put his stethoscope on her chest, he began to scream. He hollered at the nurse to start an I.V. and oxgyen.

"I remember the treatment table was too far away from the outlet for the oxgyen so he actually pushed it with his leg so the tube would reach. He just screamed . . . 'Tell Dr. MeGeehee to get here now!' "

Sharon and I were listening to every word, leaning forward with our ears and eyes wide open. Jan folded her feet under her legs on the sofa to get more comfortable. She took a deep breath and cleared her throat. Her voice turned satiny and mellow. Her eyes changed too. They looked away from us, over our heads and into another dimension. She was seeing something in her mind that Sharon and I didn't understand. Her eyes lost their color and became floating crystals, clear and free, but yet unexplainably warm.

"I've always been very afraid to die," Jan said softly, looking back at Sharon and me. "I've had a lot of illness and severe pain in my life, so I thought it must hurt awful bad to die." There was a hush in the room, even my breathing sounded loud.

"The next thing I became aware of was that I was floating. Just like leaves falling off a tree—light, airy, comfortable, very easy—and then there was this tunnel," Jan said. "And, I saw this little bitty Light way down at the end. I began to slowly approach this Light, and at some point, I no longer was the one determining whether I would approach it or not. It became like a magnet and began to pull me faster and faster." Her voice lifted, "All of a sudden, I was in the Light."

Sharon and I waited. Both of us felt anxious. My mind was going wild with images of every light I had ever seen from spotlights, to stagelights, to floodlights, to neonlights, to the natural light of day. Jan said she didn't know how to describe that Light, but it was brighter than any light she'd seen in her life. It wasn't a glaring light, but more like a glow where she didn't need to squint her eyes.

"Then I saw this young girl, and I wondered who she was. And, you want to know something really neat?" Jan smiled. "It was me! I may have grey hair now, but when I saw myself, my hair was the color it was when I was eighteen years old." Her full smile was pleasing and beautiful, and her face began to radiate. "No sooner had I discovered myself, than I saw this Personage standing a distance away from me. I wanted to see who it was. I didn't run, walk, or fly, but just like that," Jan snapped her fingers, "I was over there. All I had to do was think it!"

Jan's face and body became completely still, and there was a holy hush that filled the room. She shook her head back and forth as if she didn't know how to go on. Tears filled her eyes and spilled out the corners. Her shoulders raised up and down with deep sighs. She groaned in an effort to release what was behind her emotions. She struggled to find words to descibe what happened next.

"I knew immediately," she whispered. "I recognized Jesus Christ." Jan started weeping. She choked on the lump in her throat and used her trembling hands to wipe away the smeared makeup from under her eyes. "He never said a word, but there was complete and total acceptance of me."

For a long time, the three of us sat there in stillness. It was like we were no longer in the deep South on a hidden bayou, no longer in the USA, or for that matter, no longer on the earth but somewhere else. A place where there were no boundaries and no way to measure time. I don't know how long it was before Jan collected herself and was able to continue. When she did, she told us she was sorry for crying.

Reluctantly, she described how Jesus Christ looked. He wore a long white robe made from a thick matte-like material. The robe started at the shoulders, with big long sleeves and fell all the way down in heavy folds. His hair was brunette. His hands were strong and soft and reached out to her. There was nothing else in the environment around them, just the Light, Jesus Christ, and Jan. There were no sounds, no top, no bottom. She wasn't standing on anything and not floating either.

Once more Jan wept and apologized. Sharon and I sat in silent awe and assured her we wanted her to finish. Neither Sharon nor I had ever experienced anything like this, and we were fascinated and wanted to know as much as Jan could share.

With the sweetness of a lullaby, Jan continued, "There was so much tenderness and love and compassion and complete acceptance of me that His facial features were absolutely diminished into not even being noticable. His whole being and presence absorbed me." Big unashamed tears rolled down Jan's cheeks and when she looked up, a brilliant softness came through her entire face. She rested her eyes on Sharon and me. "And I'll tell you girls something," she said. "We need to be just like Him. We need to have so much love and tenderness exuding from us that it—doesn't—matter—what—we—look—like!"

Then she told us about looking down from above, as if she were hovering from the ceiling, and seeing two doctors and four nurses standing over her swollen body in the emergency room ordering her to breathe. They sounded like they were miles away yelling at her. Her neck was bulging clear out to her chin. She didn't want to breathe or to come back to her body and wished they would leave her alone.

"I thought to myself, *I'll breathe for you one more time, buddy, and that's all yer gettin'!*" Jan laughed. But then, she saw her dear husband standing at the foot of the bed. Bob reached out and pinched her toe. When she heard the pain in Bob's plea for her to breathe, her heart tore between staying with Jesus Christ or returning to her family. Seeing Bob, somehow she knew she must come back. Bob and her three sons needed her.

"This was not an out-of-the-body experience," Jan said quietly. "It was a death experience." The emergency room doctor looked at Bob and told him Jan's heart had stopped and that she was dead. She had been gone about fifteen minutes.

With that, Sharon and I were stunned. The impact of what we had just heard lingered. We needed to ponder and reflect on this. Sharon and I had been taken to the top of the archenemy mountain known as death and given a glimpse of what lay beyond. In an indirect way, we had sampled death, secondhand, through Jan and saw the other side through her eyes. Instead of fear, we were shown other things—mostly compassion. There was no question in our minds Jan had made the journey into the hereafter and was forever changed. Finally, I understood why Jan's eyes were laid open and unblemished. Although her human body wrestled with containing all she had experienced, her shining eyes revealed some of the sweetness she had seen on the other side.

"I do not dwell on the fact I'm going to die," she added. "You can't look at the sun all the time, and you can't look death in the face all the time, but I learned a lot from what happened to me." Sharon and I wanted her to tell us what she had learned. This was the first time we had heard ourselves, and our voices sounded earthy. Although we were adult women, Sharon and I were like the kindergartners in Sharon's class at school, full of wonder, and we needed to know.

"We are here for a purpose. It may not be anything big, but if I don't do my job, it won't get done. . . . And, for the first time in my life, I really discovered what love was." Jan paused, searching for the right words. "Love is accepting someone just the way they are and allowing them to *just be* . . . Somebody doesn't have to be what I want them to be in order to be loved. I don't have to like what people do. I don't have to like what they say, but that doesn't mean I can't love them."

She wiped away the last of her tears and sniffled. A big grin crossed her lips. The powerful emotions we felt during her story were settling down and a sense of peace surrounded us. Sharon's brown eyes were no longer bouncing with confrontations. The three of us were in one accord, but Jan had an afterglow. Her final words were as memorable as if they had been carved in stone tablets. We would always remember this day on the sleepy bayou and Jan, this woman I knew.

"We think we're always going to be here and that we have time—time—time. We take it for granted and waste valuable living time." Then, with the graciousness and the gentleness of a dove, Jan finished, "I want to make sure I tell people I love them *now*, while I've got the chance."

JAN'S SHRIMP CREOLE

Everybody told me the South was exactly where I should live because I could get shrimp so easily. We get it right off the boat, so I have as much shrimp as I can possibly eat. What you do is get an onion. Throw it in the skillet along with some green peppers. Be careful because you're only gonna cook those onions long enough to where you see through them. If you cook them any longer, forget it!

Get some cans of tomato sauce, and some cans of tomatoes. Put those in there with some Worcestershire sauce. Mix all that together. Don't tell anybody this, but then you take a half a jar of hot taco sauce and pour that in there. That's what makes it good and gives it that twang.

Let all that cook together. Add some salt. Cook for at least an hour. Then, get these little shrimp, real pink shrimp. Throw those in there. I put twice as many as you should because my boys pick 'em out. Then cook ya some rice. Rice is the staple down here in the South.

Put your cooked rice in a bowl, pour this shrimp creole over the top of it, and I'm talkin' good eatin'. I serve it with a tossed salad, French bread, and iced tea.

&. &. &.

POSTSCRIPT

HAVE YOU EVER WRITTEN a letter and then added a P.S. at the end because there was one more thing you wanted to say? Before we tell each other goodbye, please let me remind you there are other women out there, just like my seven friends in this book.

Don't be afraid to look for them or make an effort to get to know them. Women like these don't brag or boast, but they live in your neighborhood, down the road, in cities and small towns all across America and will gladly share themselves and what they know, if you only ask. Show them that you need them.

Sincerely,

Barbara

ABOUT THE AUTHOR

BARBARA JENKINS WAS BORN in Doniphan, Missouri, in the hills of the Ozark Mountains. Her family moved to nearby Poplar Bluff where she spent her childhood. Barbara graduated in 1969 from the College of the School of The Ozarks in Missouri with a B. A. in Sociology and History. She worked briefly as a high school teacher and then spent four years as a social worker in Missouri and Mississippi. In 1975 she began working on a Master's Degree at the New Orleans Baptist Theological Seminary in Religious Education.

Barbara has co-authored *The Walk West*, (Morrow, 1981) and *The Road Unseen*, (Nelson, 1985) both bestsellers. She has been a featured speaker at many conferences and conventions as well as appearing on "Good Morning America," "The 700 Club," "PTL Club," and many other TV and radio shows. Barbara presently makes here home in Nashville, Tennessee, with her three children, Rebekah, Jedidiah, and Luke.

The typeface for the text of this book is *Goudy Old Style*. Its creator, Frederic W. Goudy, was commissioned by American Type Founders Company to design a new Roman type face. Completed in 1915 and named Goudy Old Style, it was an instant bestseller. However, its designer had sold the design outright to the foundry, so when it became evident that additional versions would be needed to complete the family, the work was done by the foundry's own designer, Morris Benton. From the original design came seven additional weights and variants, all of which sold in great quantity. However, Goudy himself received no additional compensation for them. He later recounted a visit to the foundry with a group of printers, during which the guide stopped at one of the busy casting machines and stated, "Here's where Goudy goes down to posterity, while American Type Founders Company goes down to prosperity."

Substantive Editing:
Michael S. Hyatt

Copy Editing:
Darryl F. Winburne

Cover Design:
Steve Diggs & Friends
Nashville, Tennessee

Page Composition:
Xerox Ventura Publisher
Printware 720 IQ Laser Printer

Printing and Binding:
Maple-Vail Book Manufacturing Group
York, Pennsylvania

Dust Jacket Printing:
Strine Printing
York, Pennsylvania